Designing Effective Web Sites

A Concise Guide

Designing Effective Web Sites

A Concise Guide

Johndan Johnson-Eilola

Clarkson University

Houghton Mifflin Company

Boston   New York

Senior Sponsoring Editor: Suzanne Phelps Weir
Developmental Editor: Janet Edmonds
Associate Project Editor: Heather Hubbard
Production/Design Coordinator: Lisa Jelly Smith
Senior Manufacturing Coordinator: Sally Culler/Jane Spelman
Marketing Manager: Cindy Graff Cohen

Printed in the U.S.A.

Library of Congress Control Number: 2001131510

ISBN 0-618-07433-3

3 4 5 6 7 8 9-DOC-09 08 07 06

 As part of Houghton Mifflin's ongoing commitment to the environment, this text has been printed on recycled paper.

Brief Contents

Part 1: Introduction

Chapter 1 Activity: From Readers to Users in Contexts 1

Chapter 2 Users and Contexts: An Overview of Key Issues 6

Part 2: Thinking About Users

Chapter 3 Understanding Users' Contexts 21

Chapter 4 Understanding Users' Goals 33

Chapter 5 Finding out About Your Users 41

Part 3: Thinking About Structure and Layout

Chapter 6 Structures: Organizing Sites 61

Chapter 7 Pathways: Elements of Navigation 86

Chapter 8 Layouts: Formatting Pages 102

Appendix 113

Contents

Part 1: Introduction

Chapter 1   Activity: From Readers to Users in Contexts   1

Readers? Users? Audiences?   1
Who Should Use *Designing Effective Web Sites*?   2
The Scope of This Book   4
    Writing Specialized Content   4
    Instructions on Using Specific Programs   5

Chapter 2   Users and Contexts: An Overview of Key Issues   6

Thinking About Users   6
    Thinking About Structures   10
    Navigation Devices   11
    Size and Resolution   12
    Aspect Ratio   12
    Color   14
    Fixity   14
    Reading Patterns   15
    Weighing the Differences Between Print and Online   18
Exercises   19

Part 2: Thinking About Users

Chapter 3   Understanding Users' Contexts   21

    Technical Contexts   23
    Physical Contexts   27
    Mental Contexts   28
    Social and Institutional Contexts   30

Context Worksheet   31
Exercises   32

Chapter 4   Understanding Users' Goals   33

Short-Term Goals   36
Long-Term Goals   37
Conflicting and Contradictory Goals   37
Goals Worksheet   39
Exercises   40

Chapter 5   Finding out About Your Users   41

Who Are My Users?   41
Sampling: Do I Have to Talk to *All* of My Users?   42
    Random Sampling   43
    Self-Selected Groups   43
    Targeted Sampling   44
Working with Your Sample: Getting Information from Users   44
    Surveys   45
Survey Worksheet   49
    Interviews and Focus Groups   50
    Usability Testing   52
    Participatory Observation and Design   55
    Beta Testing and Post-Release Testing   58
Exercises   59

Part 3: Thinking About Structure and Layout

Chapter 6   Structures: Organizing Sites   61

Structure on ESPN's Web Site   62
Types of Structure   65
    Linear (with Scrolling)   67
Linear (with Nodes)   67
    Outline   68
    Hub and Spoke   69
Partial Network   70
    Full Network   71
Design Sketches   73
Table of Structure Types   74

Structure Worksheet   82
Exercises   84

Chapter 7   Pathways: Elements of Navigation   86

Navigational Devices   86
    In-Text Link   88
    Navigation Bar   90
    Frames   90
    Button   93
    Search Engine   94
    Forward/Backward, Up/Down, Previous/Next   95
    Table of Contents   97
    Automatic Movement   97
Navigation Device Decisions   99
Exercises   100
Projects   101

Chapter 8   Layouts: Formatting Pages   102

Exercises   110

Appendix   113

Preface
Getting Beyond Codes to Communication on the World Wide Web

Just over ten years have passed since Tim Berners-Lee, a scientist at the European particle physics center, CERN, published specifications for World Wide Web publishing. To say that the WWW has become very popular would be an understatement. Nua, an Internet research and surveying company, estimates that 407,100,000 different people accessed the Internet between September and November of 2000.

The Web offers a convenient and inexpensive means of communicating with a wide audience. Schoolchildren in the arctic regions of Nunavut publish their projects to the Web and exchange email with children at other schools (Figure 1).

Political activists at Penn State University publicize an upcoming conference on the Web, providing potential participants with information on registration, sessions, housing, and travel (Figure 2).

A loose cooperative of graduate students and teachers who study computers and writing publish *Kairos: A Journal for Teachers of Writing in Webbed Environments* (Figure 3).

Increasingly, web-based publishing has become a part of education. The Web offers students and teachers the opportunity to write not merely for each other, but for a wider audience. Although many teachers have experimented with small press runs of student material in order to gain audiences for their student work, the Web provides a much wider and deeper audience. Class work is no longer

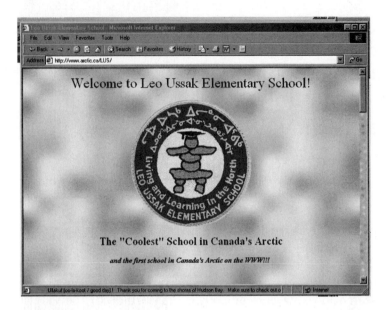

Figure 1   Main Page from Leo Ussak Elementary School, Nunavut Web site [http://www.arctic.ca/LUS], copyright © 2001. Reprinted with permission.

Figure 2   Solidarity Conference home page Web site [http://www.geocities.com/solidarityconference], copyright © 2001. Reprinted with permission.

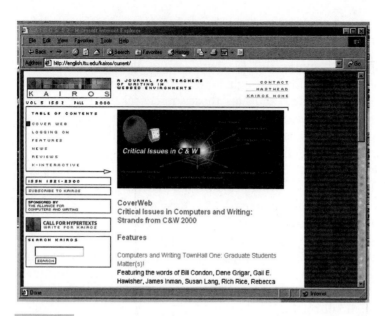

　Kairos home page Web site. Reproduced with permission from *Kairos: A Journal for Teachers of Writing in Webbed Environments* [http://english.ttu.edu/kairos].

merely a paper turned in for teacher's comments and a grade: a class assignment published to the Web is explicitly available to an audience of millions of readers.

With the opportunity comes a new set of responsibilities: publishing a document on the Web is a much more complex process than producing a word-processed term paper. Even though many of the nuts-and-bolts issues of HTML coding are now taken care of by web site design programs like Dreamweaver and FrontPage, students and teachers are still faced with the daunting task of web site *design.* Web pages and sites are potentially very different from printed pages: users move dynamically from node to node, skimming each screen with varying levels of attention, moving forward and backward. Effective web sites—ones that actually connect with readers or users in meaningful ways—must be more than single long nodes of dense text. If publishing educational projects to the World Wide Web is to become a truly useful practice—if publishing web-based course projects is to be anything more than blindly tossing documents over the wall separating the academy from the rest of the world—then students and teachers will need to learn how to define *effective* web sites.

As you might guess, this is where *Designing Effective Web Sites (DEW)* comes in. Even though there are literally hundreds of guides to creating web pages and sites, those sources take a primarily technical, functional perspective on web publishing. Invariably, they contain extensive discussions of HTML code, of image optimization techniques, or of programming issues that, while important to web publishing, detract from the real issue: how can someone design a site that's useful to another person, a site that users can navigate and read easily. Teaching someone how to design an effective web site by handing them a guide to HTML codes is like teaching someone to drive by handing them a mechanic's manual to a Ferarri: the information is interesting and important, but not to the primary point. (The Appendix to *DEW* contains references to numerous tutorials and quick-reference guides to the nuts and bolts of HTML if you need such information.)

Designing Effective Web Sites takes a broad approach to web site design, one that assumes you're interested in communicating something of importance to real people. Exactly *what* you're communicating will depend on your particular course or interests. By taking a broad perspective on web site design, *DEW* attempts to help you learn skills that will translate to other projects and other courses, or even to projects you take on in your own time. The concepts in *DEW* will work equally well for a first-year composition student publishing a critique of web-oriented advertising techniques and for a graduate student in sociology publishing research on schoolyard games.

Perhaps just as importantly, *Designing Effective Web Sites* is not intended as the primary text for any course. There are several books on the market designed as reference works for students and professionals specifically studying web site publishing and who have the time to spend a full semester or more on in-depth study of the techniques and processes of that activity. *DEW* condenses the most important aspects of professional design into a small, affordable handbook, one that can be read along with other course materials and discussions. The goal of *DEW* is to give everyone, not merely experts, the ability to design effective, usable web sites.

Though the size of *Designing Effective Web Sites* is relatively small, the task of writing *DEW* has been a long and wide-ranging process involving a number of talented and supportive people. I want to thank the hard work of my editor at Houghton Mifflin, Janet Edmonds, as well as Suzanne Phelps Weir, for her extensive support, and Heather Hubbard, who handled production. In addition, reviewers of the manuscript at various stages invariably offered comments that were perceptive as well as challenging. I would like to thank the following for helping by commenting on drafts of the manuscript:

Peter Caster
University of Texas, Austin

Michael J. Day
Northern Illinois University

Bradley Dilger
University of Florida, Gainesville

Joel A. English
Old Dominion University

E. Laurie George
University of Washington

Paula Petrik
University of Maine, Orono

Janice Walker
Georgia Southern University

In addition, students in courses I've taught over the last five years at Purdue University and Clarkson University have helped me revise and rethink my approaches to teaching web site design in important ways. Finally, my wife Kelly and daughter Carolyn remain, as always, ready with a warm smile or a word of encouragement (even when I claimed that browsing the Web was *work* not *play*). My thanks to you all.

J. J. E

Designing Effective Web Sites

A Concise Guide

1 Activity: From Readers to Users in Contexts

Objectives

- Understanding how users are different from readers or audiences
- Deciding if *Designing Effective Web Sites* will work for you

Readers? Users? Audiences?

Whom are web sites written for? This seems like a simple question, but anyone who's spent some time on the World Wide Web can testify to the fact that numerous web sites appear to have no audience beyond the author. Pages that proclaim, "Hi! This is my home page!" announce themselves to the world, but it's not clear to *whom* they're announcing themselves.

That's not to say there's anything profoundly wrong with a web site written to yourself. Consider it a first step, a "Hello, World!" that should provide the writer with the breakthrough point he or she will eventually fill with pages written to *real* people: people who will find interesting information, follow links to specialized subpages, and email the author with comments. In short, the "Hello, World!" web site should eventually transform itself into a site for **users.**

In this book, I rely heavily on the term *users*. If you're working from the theory that web sites offer text to be read, you may wonder why I don't use the term *readers*. If you're used to thinking about real-world people who work with documents, you may be more comfortable with the term *readers*. But this term doesn't get at a crucial aspect of successful, effective web sites—they are **used.** People look at the pages, skim or read them, click links, and move around the sites in ways that the more passive terms *readers* and *audiences* don't suggest.

Of course, it's possible to conceive of those terms as extremely active—numerous literary theory, feminist, and cultural studies approaches insist that readers are extremely active, contesting, revising, and inserting themselves into even the most fixed text. Still, the contortions of those theories are an attempt to wrangle traditional terms like *reader* and *audience* into a new form. Why not merely adopt a different term, one that already connotes activity and use for most users?

So for this textbook, I rely on the term *user*.

Who Should Use *Designing Effective Web Sites*?

As should be evident by the brevity of *Designing Effective Web Sites*, this text does not aim to be the definitive guide to web site authoring. Instead, I'm trying to offer a **brief** primer about major issues for new web site designers to consider—particularly, three crucial issues that new and intermediate web site designers often miss: usability, structure, and navigation. These three issues are key factors affecting whether any web site will be useful for anyone other than the author. Usability involves thinking carefully about who will be viewing your site, including issues such as how they will use the site and what they'll do with information once they find it. Structure describes how the different nodes or screens of a web site are connected to each other (and similarly determines where users can go as they move around the site). The closely related topic of navigation deals with what specific devices or facilities allow users to move from one section of a site to another.

Perhaps a quick story will make the relevance of these three topics more apparent. Jesse, a student at Enormous State University, hopes to graduate next spring semester (her parents told her seven years for her BA was long enough). After pulling out her graduation requirements sheet (which her advisor filled out for her last May), Jesse realizes she needs one more required course next semester in order to fulfill her graduation requirements.

> Jesse remembers that she had, at one point, seen an online version of the ESU's course catalog at the university web site, so she calls up the home page on her browser. The page is broken up into a number of different sections, with a

large graphic of the university's administration building in the center. On the left, she sees a list of high-level sections: Academics, Visitors, Athletics, Philanthropy. At the bottom of the screen, she sees a list of apparently miscellaneous or utility links: Calendar, Driving directions, Search, Copyright info. Jesse is frustrated to find that none of the links on the page have anything to do with classes offered next spring. She thinks about other terms that might be relevant here—courses? graduation? She remembers the Calendar link, but when she clicks it, she accesses a current-month and current-year calendar showing class start and end dates, vacations, holidays, and so on.

Panicking (how will she graduate if she can't even figure out what courses are offered?), Jesse skims again to the bottom of the page and sees the Search link. She clicks that link, which opens a search window on her screen. Into the search text field, she types "Spring 2001 courses." Her cursor changes to an hourglass and, after a five-second pause, Jesse sees a list containing titles and the first few sentences of twenty or so pages. Partway down the list, she spies Spring 2001: Tentative Course Offerings.

She clicks the underlined blue text to open the page, and at last, Jesse sees a page listing, by department, every course ESU plans on offering next semester. Luckily, as she scans down the list, she finds that the necessary course will be offered, Tuesdays and Thursdays from 12–1:30. On the printed degree requirement sheet, she copies down the dates, times, and teacher information so she can schedule the course. Then she clicks the ever-present Home button to return to ESU's home page and begins looking for graduate school application materials.

This story, or variations on it, go on every day at nearly every web site of any size. What's important about the story, for the purposes of this textbook, is how absolutely unremarkable it is: Jesse, like many users, visits a web site with a specific purpose in mind. But the designers of the ESU web site have not thought about this particular type of user, forcing Jesse to spend time digging around on the site to find a path to the information she wanted. Like many university sites (especially early ones), the ESU web site was designed for other types of users (or maybe for no particular user at all). A web site designed around usability concerns would have likely included students like Jesse as one of its primary audiences; the site designers would have asked questions of students like Jesse about how they might use a university web site.

ESU's hypothetical web site fared a little better in terms of structure and navigation: the page itself was easy to skim; that is, the information wasn't presented in dense, thick, text-heavy block but in logical sections and brief lists. And the site itself was indexed, allowing Jesse to search for the course schedule page. A better site might have offered a primary link for "students" on the home page that, when clicked, offered a more detailed list of options that students might frequently use: course schedules, open lab times, departments, financial aid, housing. By successively clicking links, Jesse could have moved slowly but surely to the information she needed.

If you've never looked for specific information on a web site, you may want to try it—it's often a frustrating experience. Jesse's difficulty in finding the information she sought may give you a better idea of why web site design is such a complicated and important issue.

Jesse's story highlights the importance of the key factors covered in this textbook: usability (making the site useful for particular types of students), structure (linking the sections of a site), and navigation (providing users with methods for getting from one point in the structure to another).

The Scope of This Book

As you see, this is a brief book. That's intentional. By leaving out some information that's best covered in other places, I've attempted to make the book quick to read and useful to a number of different audiences, including people working with different types of web site authoring programs or editors.

Writing Specialized Content

By this point, you may have asked yourself, "What about content? How do I know what to actually *put* in a web site?" Although this is a crucial question, *Designing Effective Web Sites* doesn't discuss content. I'm assuming, instead, that you're using this text as a secondary or supplemental resource, or that you already have a relatively good understanding of content. If you're in a first-year writing course, for example, you probably already had to purchase (or borrow or share) a larger textbook that contained course readings, advice about writing in general, or both. If you're in a mass media course, you've probably bought a separate mass media textbook. The same would be true for students in nearly any course—you'll purchase a separate textbook for content in that course and use *Designing Effective Web Sites* as a way to help you translate and restructure the papers or assignments you have to write in a web-based medium.

Also keep in mind that your content won't be determined completely by previously written sources like textbooks. *Designing Effective Web Sites* will also help you think about potential (and actual) users for your web site—working with those users will affect what goes into your site. Finally, early in your research for any web site, you should begin by seeing what else is already on the Web that relates to the work you're going to do: those sites will give you ideas about what sorts of information work well on the Web, about things that users want.

Instructions on Using Specific Programs

Like many users, you'll be relying on a graphical web site design program like FrontPage or Dreamweaver. *Designing Effective Web Sites* is intended to be a more general, conceptual primer on web site design issues—instruction about particular programs is best left to the documentation that came with the program. There are also numerous third-party manuals for these programs that can be bought separately. Finally, the Appendix contains links to tutorials for common web site design programs as well as HTML reference guides.

For related reasons, this textbook also doesn't cover advanced issues such as Flash authoring, JavaScript, or even basic HTML. The Appendix can point you in the right direction if you're interested in those topics; this textbook focuses on fundamental issues involved in designing simple but useful web sites.

2 Users and Contexts: An Overview of Key Issues

Objectives

- Learning how users differ from one another
- Understanding how users work within structures
- Identifying differing contextual influences on users

Designing Effective Web Sites focuses on users and structures. Understanding who will be using your web site would seem to be obviously or easily known, but many web sites are designed for completely imaginary, overly idealized users. Carefully considering who your users are—including the contexts in which they'll use your site—will help you construct a successful web site. As you think about your users, you'll also need to experiment with structures for your web site at two levels: (1) the structure of the site itself, including navigation from one screen to the next, and (2) the structure of each individual screen. Later in this book, you'll see methods for thinking about and working with potential users. You'll also investigate ways to structure your site and its individual pages so that your users will be able to successfully use your site.

Thinking About Users

Effective writing depends in fundamental ways on your ability to understand your users and their contexts. Consider, for example, two web pages on the same general topic, the Underground Railroad. In the first page (Figure 2.1), researchers at the National Underground Railroad Freedom Center site provide information on Sojourner Truth, a list of print resources for both younger and older

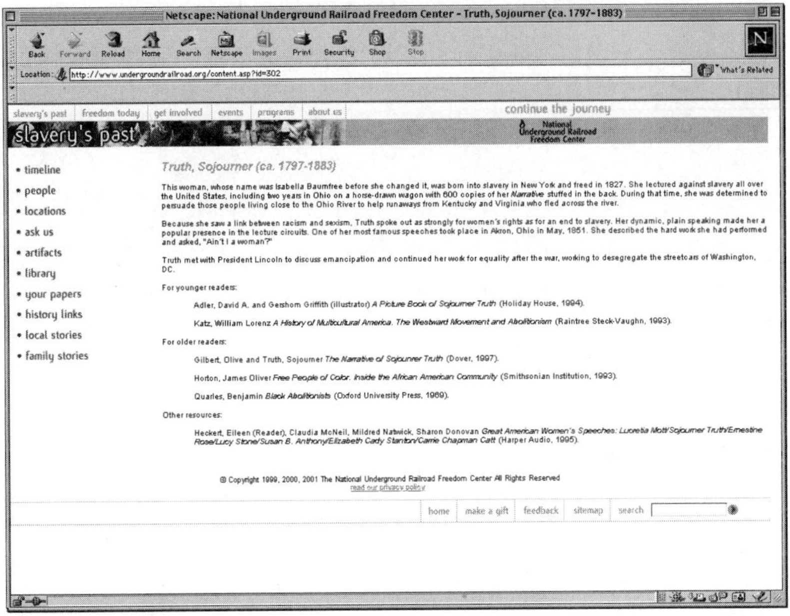

Figure 2.1   Entry on Sojourner Truth from the National Underground Railroad Freedom Center site *(Copyright © 2001 by the National Underground Railroad Freedom Center. Reprinted with permission; Netscape Communicator browser window copyright © 1999 Netscape Communications Corporation. Used with permission. Netscape Communications has not authorized, sponsored, endorsed, or approved this publication and is not responsible for its content.)*

readers, and a host of links to other sections of the large site. In the second page (Figure 2.2), designers at the PBS network provide schoolteachers with resources to integrate the television miniseries, *Africans in America,* into their classes (other sections of the site include extensive material on *Africans in America* for both general users and students).

Examine each of the pages. What types of differences in language do you see? In design? In interactivity? Each page has been crafted for different types of users in different situations. For example, in the National Underground Railroad Freedom Center site, the sentence structure and tone are designed for young adult or adult users. The

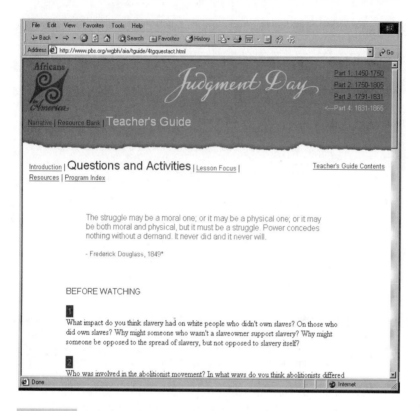

Figure 2.2   Page from the PBS web site, teacher's guide to the program
*Africans in America (From the "Africans in America" web site at
pbs.org. Coptright © 2000 WGBH/Boston)*

tone remains relatively academic, with complex sentences and a
broad vocabulary:

Truth, Sojourner (ca. 1797-1883)

This woman, whose name was Isabella Baumfree before she
changed it, was born into slavery in New York and Freed in 1827. She
lectured against slavery all over the United States, including two
years in Ohio on a horse-drawn wagon with 600 copies of her Narra-
tive stuffed in the back. During that time, she was determined to
persuade those people living close to the Ohio River to help runaways
from Kentucky and Virginia who fled across the river.

The PBS page, however, contains several different types of writing within it. Rather than simply providing information, the designers provide teachers with questions they can give directly to students in order to engage the students in discussion about the program they have watched:

> What impact do you think slavery had on white people who didn't own slaves? On those who did own slaves? Why might someone who wasn't a slaveowner support slavery? Why might someone be opposed to the spread of slavery, but not opposed to slavery itself?

Later on the PBS page (scrolled out of view in Figure 2.2), the designers not only ask such questions but also provide teachers with background materials (including an underlined hyperlink to additional material on Garnet's "Address") and concrete role-playing activities:

> The debate on Henry Highland Garnet's "Address to the Slaves of the United States" lasted for four days before Garnet's call to arms was rejected by the 1843 Negro National Convention at Buffalo. Why did delegates such as Douglass oppose the address, even though they did not oppose armed resistance? What other conflicting ideas about strategies separated the delegates? Have students research the anti-slavery positions of Douglass, Garnet, and other black abolitionists. Ask students to imagine that they are attending the convention. Have them prepare a brief speech stating their position on the views expressed in the debate.

Each site addresses different situations and different (sometimes multiple) types of users. Saying which site is better would be difficult (and perhaps pointless). In one way of thinking about the users, the designers assume users will have functionally opposite purposes for using the material on that particular page. The PBS page provides *activities or goals*; the Underground Railroad Freedom Center page provides *information*.

The PBS page provides relatively directed activities for teachers to examine and pass on to students. The designers of the page provide a small amount of context-setting material as well as occasional links to other material, but the assumption is that users will have already viewed a segment of the *Africans in America* program and will be able to use that viewing to complete the activities.

In the Underground Railroad Freedom Center page, the designers provide more general information; they assume that users are bringing some other activity or assignment with them (such as writing a historically accurate portrayal of an African American struggling towards freedom on the Underground Railroad).

As the designers of each page were well aware, understanding users and their particular contexts is fundamental to good web site writing and design. As a web site designer, you'll need to consider not merely the age of your users, but their backgrounds, educational experiences, cultures, interests, motivations, and skills. As later chapters will detail, you'll often need to work directly with your users, asking them questions about how they work and think or even asking them to work with a draft of your site to see how things go. But by devoting time and energy to this important aspect of writing, you'll learn to develop sites that work effectively for your particular users.

As later chapters will detail, you'll often need to work directly with your users, asking them questions about how they work and think, or even asking them to work with a draft of your site to see how things go. But by devoting time and energy to this important aspect of writing, you'll learn to develop sites that work effectively for your particular users.

Thinking About Structures

Although it seems obvious that printed texts are different from online texts, novice web site designers frequently begin by applying print text conventions to their web sites. The results are difficult-to-read, text-heavy sites that users try to avoid. In order to escape such disasters, you need to begin thinking about the differences between the two media; understanding the variations will help you design sites that take advantage of the unique characteristics of online media. Although there are exceptions to any generalization, print and online texts typically differ in the following areas:

- Navigation devices
- Size and resolution
- Aspect ratio
- Color

- Fixity
- Reading patterns

Navigation Devices

Web sites normally offer users a wide range of options for navigating the text. Where a print text normally offers one primary pattern of moving through the text (front to back, page by page), online texts provide multiple paths. For example, when you're reading this book, what devices does the book offer you for moving from one page to another? How do you navigate the book?

In most cases, you'll be relying on two primary devices: (1) a macrostructural pointer system such as a table of contents and (2) the microstructural system of pagination. In other words, you can skim the table of contents to find the relevant section (based on class assignment such as "Read Chapter 3 on the differences between screens and pages"). That section of the table of contents directs you to a particular page number. With that number in mind, you begin flipping the pages of the book until you arrive at the page you need. Once you start reading, you'll usually move linearly, from left page to right, turning pages in sequence until you reach the end of the assigned passage. On rare occasions, you may depart from this process to read a footnote or cross-referenced section, but in general, your print reading patterns will be largely linear.

Online texts, though, often offer a much wider range of navigational devices. In online texts such as web sites, users move around in more complex patterns. If this page were online, you might begin with the table of contents (as with the print version) in order to find the entry for the assigned reading. But rather than flip through pages to find the relevant section, you might click directly on the table of contents entry to display the text. While reading this chapter, you might move from section to section by clicking links in a navigation frame, perhaps reading the section on Resolution before the one on Color. In-text links in one of those sections might allow you to jump out of the web site altogether in order to view a site referenced as an example.

All of your movement in the site depends on navigational devices. Whereas the print text designer relies on a small number of conventional navigational devices, the web site designer will frequently want to offer users a wide range of options for moving around (and into and out of) the site. In later chapters of this book, you'll learn more about the different types of navigational devices you can use in structuring your web site.

Size and Resolution

Although the differences in size between print texts and online texts are less dramatic than they once were, in general paper offers a wider range of sizes. With printed books, in addition, readers will often be viewing side-by-side pages, doubling the effective size of the viewing area—dual-page (21-inch or larger) monitors are still relatively rare. For that matter, if you work with a computer at home, think about how your workspace looks. Is the computer sitting on a desk? When you're working on a project, do you often have books open and papers spread out next to the computer for reference while you work? Although each individual book may be smaller than the computer screen, when you fill the desk space with multiple books you'll often have a much larger area than is available on the computer screen. (In fact, this very issue is why *Designing Effective Web Sites* remains primarily a print text rather than a web text.)

Perhaps just as important, printed texts typically have a much higher resolution than screens. Whereas a professionally printed book may be printed at a resolution of several thousand dots per inch (and even inexpensive printers offer 600 dots per inch), most computer monitors offer only 72 or 75 dots per inch (Figure 2.3). The higher resolution of printed pages means increased legibility, particularly at small sizes. For example, many printed texts rely on 10- or even 8-point text sizes, which are nearly illegible on most monitors.

Although these differences might seem to make online texts a sorry substitute for print, in many circumstances online texts offer enough other benefits (such as increased navigation options) to override the size and resolution drawbacks. Careful web site designers will learn to work within—and even take advantage of—the constraints of the screen in order to build effective sites.

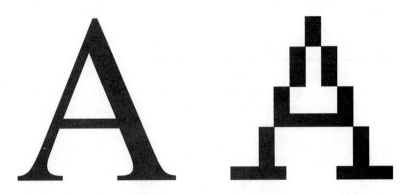

Figure 2.3   Magnified letters showing resolution differences: 1200 dots per inch (low-end professional printing) versus 72 dots per inch (standard computer monitor)

Aspect Ratio

Online texts often differ from printed texts in terms of their aspect ratio, the relative proportion of height to width of an individual page or screen. To some extent, computer screens (wider than tall) are closer to television screens than book pages (taller than wide). The aspect ratio for most computer screens (4:3) is close to that of a printed page turned on its side (3:4). Geometrically speaking, both ratios can offer the same surface space. But from a usability or readability standpoint, a wide screen cannot hold as much usable text as a tall page. As people read text across a page, their eyes tend to move up or down. If lines are too close together, their eyes begin to pick up the line of text above or below the line they are reading. In order to compensate for this tendency, designers of wide pages must insert more white space ("leading") between each line of text, reducing the number of words they can fit on a page.

However, the wider aspect ratio of the screen means that designers have more horizontal graphical space, offering designers the opportunity to display more graphics or graphics and text. Left-side or right-side navigational bars, for example, can provide readers with reminders about the overall structure of the text (listing the major sections) as well as methods for jumping from one section directly to another. (Print text readers would have to refer to a separate table of contents in order to skip around in the structure of the text.)

Color

As with size, the color available to both print and online texts varies quite a bit. However, in general, print offers a much wider range of colors than online texts do. Because print colors can be mixed, they offer printers an enormous range of colors to display on a single page. Although computer screens in theory can offer a color range much higher than print, in practice many users own screens that display far fewer colors—a few thousand or even a few hundred. The common web GIF graphics file format, for example, allows a maximum of only 256 colors. In addition, because of bandwidth concerns—the speed at which information can be downloaded—even if a user's system can display millions of colors simultaneously, designers usually want to limit the color range of images on screen in order to make web sites load quickly.

However, in everyday use, you may find it easier to use color on screen than in print. Whereas professional designers have access to high-end color printers and specialized papers, many users have access only to inexpensive color inkjet printers (which consume color ink cartridges rapidly) or monochrome laser printers. Designing on screen means access to a wider color palette than normal.

Fixity

The fixity or fluidity of online pages constitutes probably the most dramatic difference from printed pages. Printed pages are relatively fixed: once printed, they are nearly impossible to undo without destroying them. Online pages, however, are relatively fluid. Text can easily be revised during production; words and images appear and disappear on screen at will. In essence, the physical screen comprises only a glass or plastic surface covering dancing phosphor dots or diodes. As users move from screen to screen in a web site, they are literally erasing and reforming the texts as they go.

This facility allows web sites a much more dynamic nature than print texts. This feature is both a blessing and a curse. Users may delight in being able to jump around a web site but may regret their inability to find a stable ground from which to work. Designers of web sites must work hard to help users negotiate the shifting displays of information.

Reading Patterns

As you've probably already discovered, writing and reading online differs—sometimes dramatically—from writing and reading in print. Online texts tend to shift and move about as readers work with them. In fact, many theorists argue that the division between "reader" and "writer" is beginning to blur. On the face of it, this claim seems silly: when you read an online text, you're still usually reading text that someone else has written. What difference does it make if the text you're reading is composed of bits of ink on processed paper pulp or phosphor dots (or other display technology) on screen?

Good question. The difference is both subtle and simple: when you read most web pages, you're making a series of complex choices about where you go as you proceed from one screen to the next. Different readers will make different choices, each in effect constructing a slightly different, personalized text. So your reading of a particular web site will probably differ from mine; both of ours might also differ from a third person's. Obviously, the degree to which these texts differ depends on how structurally complicated a particular web site or hypertext is; the degree of structural and procedural complexity corresponds, in most cases, to the degree of "writing" each reader or user does as he or she moves through the site.

For example, in Figure 2.4, a screen from the cnet site, users can skim through a relatively complex set of categories to locate information of interest to them (19-Inch Monitors, LCDs, Options, Manufacturers, and so on). In addition, the top of the screen includes other standard categories on cnet (Downloads, Builder, Games) that users can jump to. A banner ad near the top offers users the chance to jump directly to a web-based computer hardware store in order to purchase a monitor. A search menu at the top right provides a number of choices for searching either the full cnet site or subsections. In nearly every section of this navigation-oriented (rather than content-oriented) page, users are given options for moving to new pages in (and off) the cnet site. How each user reads this individual screen, as well as what screen he or she moves to next, depends on his or her interests.

On one hand, the specific text any reader interacts with is always the "same" text—the reader is merely making choices about which parts

Figure 2.4   Complex structure in cnet site   *(Reprinted with permission from CNET, Inc., copyright 1995–2000 (www.cnet.com).)*

of the structure to read. On the other hand, the experience of reading the text will vary from one reader to the next: what each reader actually reads will depend on his or her on-the-fly decisions: one reader may be enticed by the Apple Cinema Display graphic and text, and click that link to find more about the monitor. A second reader may skim to the section offering information on 17-inch monitors in the left column, then click the link to call up a page listing all 17-inch monitor reviews. Finally, a third reader (one who knows the conventions of cnet), may search for the Editor's Pick section contained in nearly all hardware and software sections of cnet. Because this information isn't contained in the viewable part of the screen, a savvy user will scroll down the page to locate information casual users may not ever locate (Figure 2.5).

Of course, readers of print texts also make choices about what sections to read carefully, what to skim, and what to skip completely. In

Figure 2.5   Scrolling down a page in cnet to reveal additional information
(Reprinted with permission from CNET, Inc., copyright 1995–2000 (www.cnet.com).)

fact, readers of newspapers, magazines, and many technical documents jump all over the place. In fact, much of your expertise in writing and reading print texts will translate to online texts (despite many claims to the contrary, print isn't dead, it's just being transformed and augmented). Online texts accelerate many of the nonlinear, interactive tendencies of print text culture.

One might ask, "Is this a good thing?" There's not an easy answer to that question. As a reader, sometimes you'll feel you have more choices in deciding how to read a particular site or text. At other times, though, you'll feel overloaded and have a difficult time deciding where to start or where to go next. As a writer, you'll have a greater responsibility for thinking about the choices that users might want to make in working with your site. To some extent, writers no longer have as much control over readers as they used to.

Rather than limiting readers to a single path, writers are now structuring potential experiences or spaces for readers to move within.

On the far end of this trend toward blurring reader and writer responsibilities, we have interactive sites such as IRC channels and MOO spaces that allow users not only to read sites but also to write them. The ProNoun MOO at Purdue University, for example, is an interactive space that allows users (teachers and students in professional writing courses) to add nodes to a text organized around a spatial format. Participants navigate the classroom spaces to work on projects, add new "rooms" (nodes), and type messages back and forth in real time as they hold online classes. Such spaces make it clear how permeable the boundary between reader and writer is.

Weighing the Differences Between Print and Online

The rapid rush to online culture often makes us feel as if the real world—or at least print—is approaching obsolescence. But print will continue to remain a viable and useful alternative for many tasks. In some cases, print offers greater portability and flexibility, and lower cost. For example, even though online newspapers provide many useful things (searchability, rapid updating, and wide dissemination), print newspapers are still the medium of choice for most users. Print newspapers are compact, disposable, relatively high resolution, and much larger than most monitors. And the development and distribution costs of print versus online texts are more complicated than they seem at first: we talk about the Web as if it were free. It's not. Computer equipment and high-speed T1 or T3 connections enjoyed by people on many college campuses are paid for out of tuition dollars, lab fees, or subsidies.

Choosing between print and online development is a complex decision. As you work through the material in the rest of this book, keep a skeptical eye toward the features offered by online texts. Don't use features simply because they're available: think carefully about the rationale behind your choices. This text orients the web site development issue largely around users, people who will actually use the sites you develop. Let the considerations of those users drive your decisions, not the technology.

Exercises

1. Use a search engine to find three sites covering the same topic. (Hint: Pick a topic with a relatively diverse audience such as the stock market or HTML rather than a narrow topic such as a sports team.) Use the table to evaluate how each site deals with the context and needs of its particular audience.

	Site 1	Site 2	Site 3
Who uses the site?			
Where are they?			
What do they want from the site?			
How does the text of the site address the users?			
How do the graphic elements of the site address the users?			

2. Find a site that is designed for a highly specific audience (sports nuts, software engineers, a particular music group). How does the language (structure and terminology) suit that particular audience? Do you think they visit the site for specific reasons? If relative novices wished to learn about the topic covered by the site, how might the language of the site differ? Attempt to revise the site to deal with this new audience.

3. Using a site you found in Exercise 2, have classmates visit the site. Ask them to talk to you about their experiences, or observe them visiting the site and talking through their reading, comments, and questions as they go. What information does this give you about the site and possible revisions?

4. Visit your school's web site. Can you identify ways that the designers have addressed different users or different activities on the same page? How many specific audiences can you identify just by looking at the main page of the site? Does the site offer information not only for students like you but also for visitors? Alumni? Parents? Other groups?

5. Find a newspaper that has both a print and an online format (your campus newspaper, a local or even a national or international publication).

Compare the print to the online version. Does each have similar coverage? What things are present in one but not in the other? Why? Which format would you rather use?

6. Find examples of several different types of print documents: a magazine article, a short story, an encyclopedia article, a textbook chapter. If you redesigned these texts for web-based reading, what other texts might you link them up to? Think like an interested reader: while you are reading the magazine article, what other things might you be interested in finding out while you read?

7. Find a local phone book. List in writing (online or by hand) the following items:

   ■ What specific information are you normally looking for? (Be specific. It might help to think of an actual example of the last time you used a phone book. Were you looking for a person's name? A type of service? Other information?)

   ■ When you opened the book, what did you begin looking for? Just as important, how did you *know* what you were looking for? Experience?

   ■ Where on the page you opened did you look first? How did you move around on the page?

   ■ Did you move to another page? Did you skim? What things did you read when you skimmed?

   ■ How long did you take to find the information you needed?

   ■ When you found the information, what did you do with it? Write it down? Memorize it? How did you use it? After you used it, did you remember the information or make a copy of it so you could find it later?

   ■ What do these things tell you about how the phone book was structured?

8. Look with a critical eye at the space you normally use for working with a computer. How does that physical space structure your work? For example, is it designed to discourage working with another person on a collaborative project, or is it set up primarily as an individual space? Is there room to spread out other materials (print textbooks, papers, and so on)? How is the room lit? How loud or quiet is it? (And perhaps as important, does the sound level in the room correspond to the sound level *you* want?) Are you allowed to have a cup of coffee? If you could design the "perfect" work area for your computer, what would it look like?

3 Understanding Users' Contexts

Objectives

- Understanding how technology influences users

- Understanding how physical location influences users

- Understanding how mental states influence users

- Understanding how social and institutional contexts influence users

Outside a particular context, communication has no meaning. This might seem a silly claim—along the lines of "If a tree falls in the forest and no one is there to hear it, does it make a sound?" However, if you stop to think about how the meaning of words changes from one context to another, you'll start to see how important context is to communication and meaning. For example, take the simple phrase "Keep it down." In a noisy room, it can be used as a command—but only by someone with the authority to issue a command. In an already quiet room, it can be seen as a sarcastic comment (issued, for example, by a teacher who has just told her class to discuss something—the fact that they're still quiet means they're not yet working). The sentence might also be used in a hockey game by a referee (who is warning the left wing to keep his stick down) or a goalie (who is pleading with his defenseman to knock an airborne puck down to make it easier to handle). You can create a nearly infinite set of meanings for the simple sentence by varying the context. The same is true as different users or readers move in and out of contexts—novices will find technical jargon meaningless, whereas experts will find lay terminology far too vague to be useful.

Designing effective, professional web sites demands that you understand and plan for the contexts in which web sites will be used. You'll need to think carefully about how to deal with different contexts. This chapter discusses context and sets the stage for effective design; later chapters provide strategies for finding out more about particular contexts by working directly with users.

Keenan sees an ad for a new local coffeehouse in the student newspaper and considers taking his friend Marty to lunch for Marty's birthday. Unfortunately, the ad doesn't list prices for anything. Keenan's a little short on cash this week, and he wants to make sure he's not overspending. But Keenan spies a URL in the ad and thinks that the web site for the coffeehouse may include a menu. He opens up a browser window on the computer in his apartment, enters the address of the web site, and waits. And waits. And waits. Looking at the progress bar on the bottom of the screen, Keenan is dismayed to see that the page is loading a file called background.jpg, with only 10 percent of the 2.5MB file loaded. At this rate, Keenan realizes his modem is going to take nearly ten minutes to load what is probably just a fancy background graphic. The designers of the web site apparently didn't test the page before they put it online, or if they did test it, they used a fast Ethernet connection rather than a 56K modem.

Luckily, Keenan's savvy enough to know that he can speed things up by turning off the "load images automatically" in his browser. After disabling the images, Keenan reloads the web site (now going on five minutes in what he thought would be a thirty-second procedure). Success! The page loads quickly, although it's a little dull without the graphics. And difficult to understand—apparently, many of the key elements on the page (like the title of the restaurant) are **only** in graphics. Keenan scrolls up and down the page a few times, trying to guess which link to click to find a menu. After seven or eight missteps, he loads a page that has names of dishes and prices on it. The food looks good and the prices are in range, but then Keenan remembers that his friend Marty is a pretty strict vegetarian; all the dishes Keenan sees have meat in them. Disgusted with the whole process—nearly ten minutes after he started—Keenan closes the browser window and decides to buy Marty a CD instead. (The coffeehouse actually had a vegetarian section, but it was on a separate page; links to it were graphics rather than text, so Keenan never saw them.)

Technical Contexts

As many designers have found out, two users with different technical setups can display the same web site with dramatically different results. Netscape Navigator displays the same code differently than Internet Explorer, both of which will display much differently than Lynx, a text-only browser. The technical context can have a large impact on how pages look and even if they load at all, particularly if designers draw on newer features.

Consider the main page of a relatively simple site, Yahoo, in Internet Explorer compared to Lynx (Figures 3.1 and 3.2).

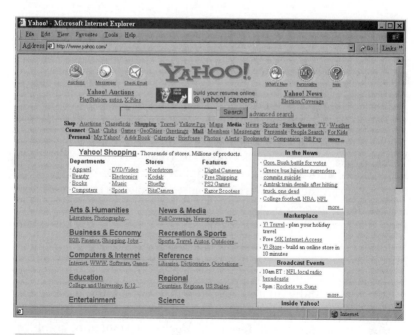

Figure 3.1   Yahoo web site viewed in Internet Explorer browser. *(Reproduced with permission of Yahoo! Inc. © 2000 by Yahoo! Inc. YAHOO! and the YAHOO! logo are trademarks of Yahoo! Inc.)*

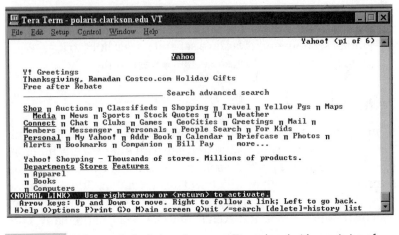

Figure 3.2   Yahoo web site in Lynx browser. *(Reproduced with permission of Yahoo! Inc. © 2000 by Yahoo! Inc. YAHOO! and the YAHOO! logo are trademarks of Yahoo! Inc.)*

At a slightly subtler level, even relatively similar browsers such as Internet Explorer and Netscape Communicator will display the same information differently. Look at the Clarkson University web site in Figure 3.3.

Although the page displays more or less in the same layout when viewed in Internet Explorer, detailed views illustrate variations between the ways each browser handles pop-up text and spacing between graphics fill-in boxes. Notice, in Figure 3.4 (p. 26), the additional space above the search box in the Netscape display at left. In addition, examine the differences between how the column of text (indicating subsection options corresponding to the Student button) displays. This text, which appears on screen when users position the cursor over main category buttons, changes as the mouse hovers over different buttons. As each browser displays the text, it formats the text differently, with text in the Netscape Communicator version scrolling off the page, and text in the Internet Explorer version flowing into the graphic in the center of the page. Although these may seem subtle differences, precise placement of graphics and text is a crucial matter. For example, if the graphic were much

Figure 3.3   Clarkson University web site in Netscape Communicator. *(Reprinted with permission of Clarkson University, Potsdam, N.Y.)*

closer to the button column, the pop-up text might be completely illegible in Internet Explorer.

At a more dramatic level, you may find that advanced features are supported differently by browsers, as I discovered when I attempted to view a course syllabus page in Netscape Communicator in front of my class—the page had displayed fine with Internet Explorer, but Netscape Communicator had problems finding the external stylesheet I had used to structure the page (Figure 3.5, p. 26). In theory, the missing stylesheet should have meant only that the page displayed with slightly different fonts.

And we haven't even touched on web-enabled cell phones, Palm Pilots, or WebTV systems. If you suspect these users will be in your target audience, you'll need to design pages to address their technical capabilities.

INFORMATION FOR:
CURRENT STUDENTS
PROSPECTIVE STUDENTS
FACULTY/STAFF
ALUMNI
CORPORATE CONNECTION

OR SELECT FROM:
ATHLETICS
DIRECTORY
SITE MAP
VISITORS CENTER

SEARCH

Student Life
Calendar
Student
Administrative
Services
Library
Academics
Class
Materials
On-line
Campus
Information
Services
Career Center
Student
Affairs
Residence
Life
Athletics
Dining
Bookstore
Student
Guidebook
Student Web
Pages
Catalog

INFORMATION FOR:
CURRENT STUDENTS
PROSPECTIVE STUDENTS
FACULTY/STAFF
ALUMNI
CORPORATE CONNECTION

OR SELECT FROM:
ATHLETICS
DIRECTORY
SITE MAP
VISITORS CENTER

SEARCH

Student Life
Clarkson This Week
Student Administrative Services
Library
Academics
Class Materials On-line
Campus Information Services
Library
Career & Professional Development
Athletics
Services
Dining
Bookstore
Student Guidebook
Parents Association
Student Web Pages
Catalog

Figure 3.4   Detail of Clarkson University web site displayed in Netscape Navigator (left) and Internet Explorer (right). *(Reprinted with permission.)*

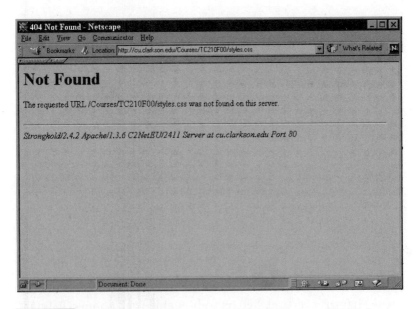

Figure 3.5   "Not Found" error when attempting to load page with stylesheet link improperly configured for Netscape Navigator. *(Reprinted with permission.)*

As you design web sites and talk to potential users, be sure to begin constructing a picture of the technical setups your users may have. An internal site used on a company's intranet may allow you to know exactly what hardware, software, and configuration each user will have, particularly if that company maintains tight control over the configuration. (In some companies, employees will have a standard set of hardware and software installed, but they may then reconfigure it on their own—changing browsers, monitor settings, or even hardware—so make sure you double-check any assumptions about "standard" configurations.) However, if you're designing a site that will be read by a variety of users, you'll have to think about the major variations in their setups. In some cases, particularly if you are using cutting-edge (or, more accurately, "bleeding edge") code in your site, you may find it necessary to design multiple pages that load for different browsers.

Further, unless you are sure of the physical capabilities of all of your users, you should keep in mind accessibility for disabled users who may have difficulty reading small text sizes or images. In some cases, for example, blind users may rely on a screen-reading program that speaks the words on the page out loud. If you're using images for key information, those users will never get that information. In most cases, you'll be able to include features you want while not locking out other users, provided you do things like include <ALT> tags that describe your image in the code for the image. You can find extensive discussion and tips on methods for designing web sites for accessibility at sites such as http://www.cast.org/bobby/ (the site also includes a program that will read and evaluate your web pages to check for common accessibility problems).

Physical Contexts

Stop for a moment and listen. What do you hear? Classmates talking or whispering? Music from your CD player turned down low? Or cranked to 11? Your physical location affects how you read, write, and think. Your context—noises you hear, the environment (hot or cold, windy or calm), people, and the activities going on around you—affects how you process information. For example, if you're the sort of person who needs peace and quiet to work on a paper, you'll find it difficult—maybe even impossible—to write in a noisy, crowded room. On the opposite end of the spectrum, some people find they absolutely have to have noise in order to work productively.

In addition to obvious things like noise, the things around you affect how you work and think. If you're in a large, social group of people, you'll probably experience problems focusing on a task like reading extensive text on a computer screen; instead, you'll be apt to engage in conversations with those around you. When you do turn your attention to the screen, you'll find that other people may look over your shoulder or sit next to you and begin participating in the activity you once did solo.

The physical location of users, then, affects how they use web sites. If you're designing a site for a public-access kiosk or touch-screen display, you'll want to design texts with large, flashy displays and minimize extensive blocks of small text. In such situations, you may even find that you want to offer choices or prompts for discussion, so users can talk to each other and mutually engage with the site—a well-designed site can turn a distraction into a strength. If, however, you know that your users will be in quiet, private surroundings, you may be able to increase the amount of text you use, knowing that their attention span and focus will be up to the task. (But be aware that the physical context is only one factor in the equation; other factors, like mental contexts and social and institutional contexts, will affect a user's ability to focus.)

Mental Contexts

The mental context—more commonly referred to as mental state—affects how people use a site. Consider, for example, a person who suspects he or she has a fatal but undiagnosed disease reading a medical information web site such as drkoop.com. The page about tuberculosis (Figure 3.6) lists the following symptoms:

Initially not apparent, or limited to minor cough and mild fever

Fatigue

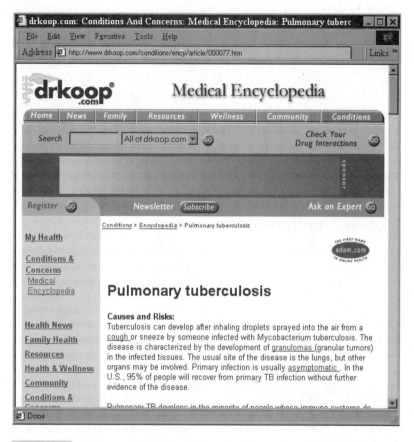

Figure 3.6 drkoop medical information web site *(Reprinted with permission of drkoop.com, Inc.)*

Weight loss

Coughing up blood

Slight fever and night sweats

What might have happened to nervous users if those symptoms had been listed first? In order to prevent people from jumping the gun, the designers of the drkoop.com web site have put more general information near the top, encouraging users to read the full article.

The article avoids playing down the seriousness of the disease—if there's a chance that users may be suffering from tuberculosis, they should seek professional medical advice immediately.

Although users could still skip all the general information and scroll immediately to the end, designers have a responsibility to make reasonable efforts to encourage readers to use information wisely.

Similarly, users who are relaxed work differently than those who are excited, and both of these types of users work differently than someone suffering from mental exhaustion.

Social and Institutional Contexts

Nearly as important as all other contexts are the social and institutional contexts in which users are working. To return to an earlier example, if you were at a party, even if you **could** get people to talk quietly and not read over your shoulder, how likely is it that you would **want** to work? The social context that you're in discourages you from using the computer to quietly browse serious web sites. Likewise, you've probably been in public labs, computer-equipped classrooms, or workspaces in which the tranquil atmosphere was pierced by a sound clip blaring from the speakers of someone's computer. That's not to say that someone working in an office would never browse a recreational web site—in fact, people commonly do. But most people also understand that a workplace or classroom context is not quite appropriate for viewing all types of web sites (in fact, serious legal problems can stem from viewing sites in a public lab or classroom that offend other users with the display of pornographic images).

Institutional and social contexts are not merely limiting devices, but suggestive ones as well. A user working in a library on a research paper may be more likely to read carefully and critically, to bookmark important sites and copy passages of text to a notes file. And an engineer selecting appropriate materials for an important project is likely to be willing to read carefully (whereas the user of an entertainment site might hit the back button as soon as he or she sees a page with no graphics and full of small text). When you think about your users, take into account not only their physical surroundings and mental state but also their social or institutional environment.

Context Worksheet

Technical Contexts	
Do all the users have exactly the same equipment? If so, how does it affect what you can put on the web site?	
Will you need to use cutting-edge coding?	
Can you accommodate users with disabilities? (Have you used an accessibility checklist?)	
Physical Contexts	
Are the users in a noisy or quiet environment?	
Are they comfortable?	
Mental Contexts	
Are the users in a hurry, or do they have time to read?	
Will the users be distracted by things around them or events in their life?	
How important is the information on the web site to them?	
Social and Institutional Contexts	
Are people around them engaged in similar tasks?	
Are the users visiting the web site to find information they have been assigned to find or make decisions with?	
Will they be rewarded (with pay or with high grades) for reading the web site carefully?	

(continued)

Other Considerations	
Will you need to fill out more than one version of this worksheet for identifiable groups of users (for example, teachers and students for an educational web site)?	
Are there users whom you won't be able to accommodate no matter what you do? Are there other methods (besides web sites) to get information to them?	

Exercises

1. Using an accessibility checklist such as the one at http://www.cast.org/bobby/, review and take notes on your findings from three different home pages:

   ■ Your university

   ■ A major television network

   ■ The AARP (http://www.aarp.org/)

   Which sites did the best? Which did the worst?

2. Take one of your textbooks to a party. Read the textbook. In a notebook, record your experiences. How did people react? How difficult was it to read? How did you feel?

3. Find out if your university or employer has an "appropriate use" policy for web browsing. Are there activities that are forbidden?

4 Understanding Users' Goals

Objectives

- Evaluating users' short-term goals

- Figuring out users' long-term goals

- Weighing conflicting goals

Users will come to your web site with a variety of goals, sometimes even conflicting ones. In order to make your web site most effective, you'll have to find out what those goals are for your intended (and sometimes unintended) users. You can use this information to make decisions about content, structure, and navigation as well as writing style and textual rhetoric.

For example, users come to a site such as Microsoft's main web page (Figure 4.1, p. 34) for a very wide range of goals. Some people are looking for software upgrades, some are looking for announcements about products, some are looking for employment possibilities. These very different goals are managed by the designers of the web site through a variety of methods. Later in this book you'll learn how to address different goals and needs in a web site. Your first step, however, is to figure out what those goals **are.**

Users typically have both local and global goals: things they want to do immediately (for example, when they scan a page, what are they looking for?) and things they want to do over the long term (for example, learn how to design a web site). These two levels are relative rather than absolute and, in fact, can cascade into a nearly infinite series of goals. And as the Microsoft page shows, as a web site designer, you can also attempt to *affect* what the users want to do by

Figure 4.1   Main page on Microsoft's web site *(Screen shot reprinted by permission from Microsoft Corporation.)*

offering options, such as urging them to purchase merchandise on-line. Remember that as a designer you are not a passive vessel through which messages flow—you're an active agent, negotiating meanings with users.

A user visiting a web site to get information about Habitat for Humanity (Figure 4.2) might be part of a larger goal to join a workcrew putting up a home. In these cases, the user's local goal is information seeking. And even long-term goals can themselves become components of larger long-term goals; for instance, joining a Habitat workcrew might be part of a New Year's resolution to give something back to the community or to help others. In Figure 4.2, given the user's local goal of getting information about joining a work crew on a Habitat project near his or her home, the user would probably quickly locate the link Find Your Local Habitat Affiliate.

Figure 4.2   Habitat for Humanity home page *(© 2001 Habitat for Humanity International.)*

This link would then take the user to a page that allows him or her to list local affiliates by U.S. state or zip code, or to find locations outside the United States. The lists contain content information and, in some cases, local web sites the user can use to track down the information he or she needs—how to join a local workcrew. Users who come to the site with specific short-term goals such as donating funds will find the link they need; users who come with only a vague long-term goal, like "Help out those less fortunate," will begin structuring and restructuring potential short-term goals as they skim across the page, reading text and viewing images. As you can see, web sites such as this work hard to answer both short-term and long-term goals.

Short-Term Goals

Short-term goals are among a user's most immediate needs when he or she is reading a screen of text. As the name implies, short-term goals are usually accomplished in a short amount of time, seconds to minutes. For this reason, it's crucial that web sites help users accomplish short-term goals quickly. Notice that the initial page of the Habitat web site doesn't even attempt to answer the hypothetical (but likely) user's short-term goal of finding a local project to work on—it would be information overload if the splash page of the Habitat web site listed every Habitat project for every local affiliate. But what the site does is *start* to answer the question by having an easily visible link to the local affiliates search page. So what's important is not that the main page address every potential goal a user might have, but that the page start to answer the question. If you think visitors to your web site will have questions that are too complex to address, at least try to get them on the track to an answer, even if it will take a little while for them to reach their destination.

Avoid forcing users to click an apparently endless series of links—after three or four clicks, many users will give up. Short-term goals are about either finding immediate answers or, at the very least, making reasonable progress. If the user's short-term goal ends up being complicated, the web site designer will have to convince the user that what he or she has is really a long-term goal. Think, for example, of computer programs that promise would-be web site developers "professional-looking sites in just minutes." Certainly this is an attractive notion because it collapses a very complicated long-term goal (designing an effective, professional web site) into a short-term goal (clicking a few buttons). A more effective—and successful—approach is to convince users that their overall goal represents a complicated undertaking, one that can be achieved only by completing a series of shorter-term goals.

Long-Term Goals

Long-term goals represent relatively large, complicated things, often themselves components of even larger long-term goals. For example, designing an effective web site for your student organization or your employer is a long-term goal comprising various short-term goals (interview potential users, map goals, draw tentative structure, import existing text into HTML, and the like). As you enter into that project with your long-term goal, you begin a successive process of breaking down the goal into shorter elements. If you have a great deal of experience with a long-term goal, you may not even have to think about how to decompose that goal into short-term items; you've done it so frequently the process is nearly automatic. (Think about the first time you sent an email message versus the most recent time—you've probably gotten much better and quicker at it.)

From another perspective, your long-term goal of designing an effective web site for a specific project probably relates to even larger long-term goals. A good web site for your student organization might, for example, increase membership in your organization and revitalize a flagging participation rate; it might also be part of your overall personal career goal of gaining experience in real-world projects in order to flesh out your resume and, in turn, secure yourself a great job in a year. (Goals are often multiple—there's no reason users can't satisfy multiple goals with a single action.)

Conflicting and Contradictory Goals

In real-world situations, goals often don't sort out into neat, linear packages. Users come to web sites looking for a piece of information and get distracted, follow links that weren't part of their original goal, get lost, and so forth. In some cases, users will come to a site with contradictory goals. Let's say you're doing research for a course project on the Web on a Saturday autumn afternoon. You're using the search engine AltaVista® to track down possible suppliers for fender materials your team needs as part of an automotive engineering product design class (Figure 4.3).

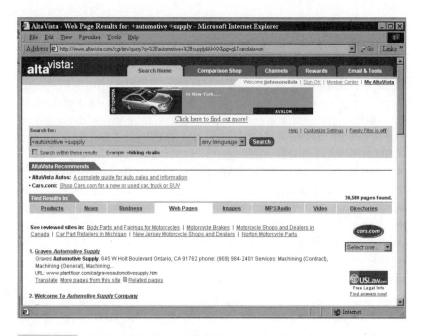

Figure 4.3   AltaVista® search results page (after searching on "+automotive
+supply"). *(Copyright © 2000 AltaVista® Company. All Rights
Reserved; Courtesy Toyota Motor Sales, U.S.A., Inc.)*

But your "official" short-term and long-term goals (which involved
typing "+automotive +supply" into the search engine box) conflict
with another set of goals, those that are thinking about getting outside for a hike. Like many search engines, AltaVista® offers free
services to users based on an advertising model: the designers hope
you'll click on links so that they can register "click-throughs" that are
then used to bill the sponsors whose links are selected. With three
clicks and typing in your zip code, you're quickly following a new set
of long- and short-term goals, at the Weather Channel's web site
(Figure 4.4).

At this point, noting the forecast, you assess your situation and
may decide to head back to AltaVista® and your previous set of
goals.

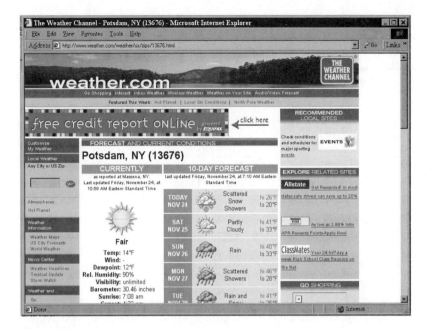

Figure 4.4   Weather Channel page for local weather in Potsdam, NY. *(Copyright © 2000 by The Weather Channel Enterprises, Inc. Reprinted with permission.)*

Goals Worksheet

Goals Worksheet	
Organization or person the site is for.	
Primary user of the site (fill out additional worksheets for multiple, primary audiences).	
Why would that user come to this site?	
List his or her short-term goals.	
List his or her long-term goals.	

(continued)

Do the short-term and long-term goals naturally connect? Or do they conflict?	
Will you have to help the user revise his or her goals? (Are his or her expectations skewed?)	
Does this user's goals conflict with other primary users' goals?	

Exercises

1. Come up with a question related to your classes or degree. Write your question out in the form of a goal. Then, keep a log of your experiences attempting to locate an answer to your question by visiting your school's web site. Were you able to find an answer? Did you have to backtrack?

   Followup: Do you think that you *should* have been able to find an answer to your question more quickly? Or was the question too specialized to deal with at the topmost levels of the web site?

2. Assume that you want to write an email message to your instructor asking her to change your grade on the last assignment. As you sit down with your email program, ask yourself what your goals are, both short term and long term. How well does the email program address your short-term goals? What about your long-term goals? Can you think of ways to improve the program for users like you?

3. Fill out a goals worksheet for one of the following web sites. Feel free to examine related web sites (similar sites in different areas, competitors' sites, and the like).

   - A local women's shelter that offers shelter and counseling for victims of domestic abuse
   - A school's student organization for a particular interest or hobby (take your pick)
   - A high school biology teacher
   - A student team project competing in a national competition (for instance, SunRayce, Concrete Canoe)

5 Finding out About Your Users

Objectives

- Deciding who your users are
- Choosing an appropriate method for sampling
- Figuring out how to get information from users

In order to design sites that are valuable to your users, you're going to have to develop methods for finding out more about who will be using your site. For an extremely simple site, you might be able to get away with just thinking, but in many cases you're going to need to support careful thinking with some hard data. There's no substitute for actually talking to your users—not all of them in most cases, but at least good representatives of the population who can give you insight into their needs, expectations, and abilities.

Who Are My Users?

Finding out about your users requires that you first figure out whom your web site is designed for. Sometimes that's more difficult than it sounds—frequently, people design web sites without thinking in concrete terms about their audience.

As you begin to think about your users, you first need to determine **who** they are and **where** they are. This seems like a silly question—who would design a web site without knowing who their users would likely be?

In reality, the intense cultural buzz surrounding the rise of the World Wide Web has caused many organizations and individuals to throw up a web site in order to define a "web presence." Unfortunately, this process often results in a public image as cloudy and unusable as a sink full of dirty dishwater: pages with pointless hit counters, dizzying tiled background patterns, and more. Some of these sites are forgivable and understandable errors—unless you've spent some time thinking carefully about web site usability and design issues for your audience, it's easy to head off in the wrong direction. (But if you really do want to see some of these sites, visit Vincent Flanders' site at http://www.websitesthatsuck.com/. Don't say I didn't warn you.)

In order to design an effective, targeted web site, you'll first have to figure out who your users are, which is an issue of context, as discussed in Chapter 3. The discussion and worksheets in the current chapter assume that you've already determined your primary and secondary audiences and their various contexts. The remainder of this chapter provides you with some methods for working with your users to gain better information about them. Don't lose sight of the fact that as you communicate more with your users, you'll probably find that your audience and context analyses have shifted—be sure you update as you go along.

Sampling: Do I Have to Talk to *All* of My Users?

If your site has more than a handful of users, your first question will probably be, "Do I have to talk to *all* of my users?" The short answer, luckily, is "No—just a subset." You'll be able to select a small group of users to work with; in some cases, you'll work with that smaller set for quick things like surveys, then pick an even smaller subset for more in-depth discussion, such as interviews or usability studies (both discussed later).

The tricky part of this is deciding **who** that small group (and smaller group) is. You'll need to sample your potential audience, using one of a variety of methods: random sampling, self-selected groups, or targeted sampling (there are other methods for scientifically sampling populations, but these three will be good rough starts for nearly any web site project).

Random Sampling

Random sampling sounds very simple: you randomly pick people from a group and assume that information you get from them represents that of the larger group. Unfortunately, it's very difficult to come up with a truly random sample. Some groups won't respond to your questions, some groups will be more vocal than others, and so on. The familiar photo of just-elected Harry S Truman holding aloft the "Dewey Defeats Truman" headlined newspaper provides an important example of sampling error. The erroneous newspaper prediction was based on poll data gathered by calling voters to ask whom they'd voted for in the presidential election. When a sizable margin reported that they'd voted for Dewey, the newspaper felt confident that they could project the winner. Unfortunately, the pollsters neglected to take into account the fact that many voters in that era didn't have telephones—in the final tally, those voters cast their lot with Truman in a large enough margin to swing the vote. Other problematic issues with random sampling include bias (the person doing the sampling being predisposed to talk more to one part of the group than to others), statistical sample size errors (not selecting enough users to give you an accurate overall picture), and outliers (missing key users who are a minority but have strong or important information).

That's not to say that random sampling can't be a useful tool, only that you need to be aware of its limitations. Often, relatively random sampling is used to augment other methods.

Self-Selected Groups

Self-selected groups are those that choose to participate in your survey, interview, or other audience information-gathering activity. This method is useful because your users tend to be interested in the topic and willing to talk with you or fill out surveys. More and better information means a better web site, right? Sort of. What about those who **don't** select themselves to participate in your research? Often, those people are crucial elements of your audience; they just don't (for various reasons) choose to participate. Like random sampling, self-selected sampling can offer an important channel for information and feedback, provided you use it along with other methods.

Targeted Sampling

Targeted sampling does just what the name implies. You think carefully about your overall group of users or potential users (as part of the analysis in Chapters 3 and 4) and then make sure you get input from members in the representative groups. If, for example, you're designing a web site for your community food bank, your primary audiences may be potential donors, other community agencies (for instance, the women's shelter that may refer clients to a food bank), and potential clients. In targeted sampling, you would attempt to work with at least a few people in each of those groups. In addition, inside each group, you would want to think about differences in each of the subgroups. For example, when you look at potential donors, you might first think of "average" citizens and ask your roommates if they'll agree to be interviewed. And, certainly, your roommates may be part of the food bank web site audience—but will they accurately represent that whole potential donor audience? What about families in the community (many of whom may have higher disposable incomes than college students and, therefore, food in their pantries that they could conceivably donate)? For that matter, what other agencies might donate food? Would the food bank be willing to serve as a link between local caterers and restaurants (many of which have unopened trays of food that would otherwise be discarded after events) and local shelters?

As you can see, your sampling process is actually also recursive, like most good design processes—you may begin changing your audience and web site goals on the fly.

Working with Your Sample: Getting Information from Users

Once you've decided who your users are, you have to come up with ways to get information from them. In some cases, after you've done some work with users, you may decide to get a different sample. Working recursively is a good strategy for ensuring you get the best information possible from the right users. There are many methods for getting your sample of users to talk with you; select the method that seems most appropriate to the types of users you have, the goals for your web site, and the type of information each method gives. The methods are not mutually exclusive; a careful designer will normally use multiple methods to get a better picture of who the site's users are and how they'll use the site.

Surveys

Surveys offer a way to get quick feedback from users. Typically, you would ask users to answer a series of multiple-choice, Likert-scale, true or false, or short-answer questions to gather information.

The structure, size, and location of your survey will depend on your specific needs. Think carefully about the questions in the survey so that you'll gather the sort of information you need. Think also about how willing your audience will be to take the time to complete the survey. Although you may identify thirty things you want to know about the users, would you be better off paring that down to ten, quickly answered questions, leaving the rest to interviews with a smaller number of users?

If you're using surveys to generate data about a completely new site, you'll need to find some way to distribute the survey to your sampled audience. If you're working with a client or employer, see if there's some place where a relatively random group is gathered, like a class that you could visit to distribute and then collect the quick survey. If that's not feasible, can you email the survey to a small group? (Be careful about sending unsolicited email, though, especially to groups you're not already familiar with. People frequently view unsolicited messages as an intrusion. But if a supervisor or manager agrees, for example, to give you the email addresses of a small group of employees, you could send them the survey with a kind request to participate—and be sure to let the group know that their supervisor thought the survey was important enough to have them fill it out.) Better yet, have the supervisor or teacher distribute the survey directly.

Figure 5.1 Opening screen for survey on WebReview.com site *(Reprinted with permission of CMP L.L.C, WebReview.com, Manhasset NY. All rights retained by CMP Media LLC.)*

If you're looking for feedback on an already running web site (or have access to a web site that deals with the same audience as the one you're going to work with), you can integrate pop-up windows that offer users the opportunity (self-selected) to fill out a brief survey. The example shown in Figure 5.1, from the industry resource WebReview, also offers the added incentive of a prize.

If users agree, they're taken to a brief survey (Figure 5.2). (Note that survey users who have a concrete interest in finishing—in this case,

Figure 5.2   Welcome message on WebReview.com survey *(Reprinted with permission of CMP L.L.C, WebReview.com, Manhasset NY. All rights retained by CMP Media LLC.)*

to win the American Express gift certificate—are more likely to fill out longer surveys.) This survey, like many surveys, is run by someone other than WebReview.com—perhaps a firm that has paid WebReview for the right to pop up the survey because they know WebReview's users are similar to their own customers. (Clients also have an interest in the effectiveness of the web site, but often don't understand how crucial usability testing and user feedback are.) The survey begins with a brief explanation of the survey. This is a very important feature because it lets the users know what the information will be used for.

After clicking the right arrow, users come to the body of the survey, which proceeds question by question (Figure 5.3, p. 48). Early questions on surveys frequently involve finding out what part of the audience the user belongs to; this is particularly important for helping you sort tendencies for particular subgroups (and also lets you see if one group isn't being represented).

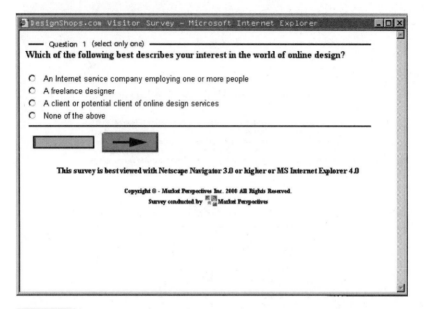

Figure 5.3   Question 1 in WebReview.com survey *(Reprinted with permission of CMP L.L.C, WebReview.com, Manhasset NY. All rights retained by CMP Media LLC.)*

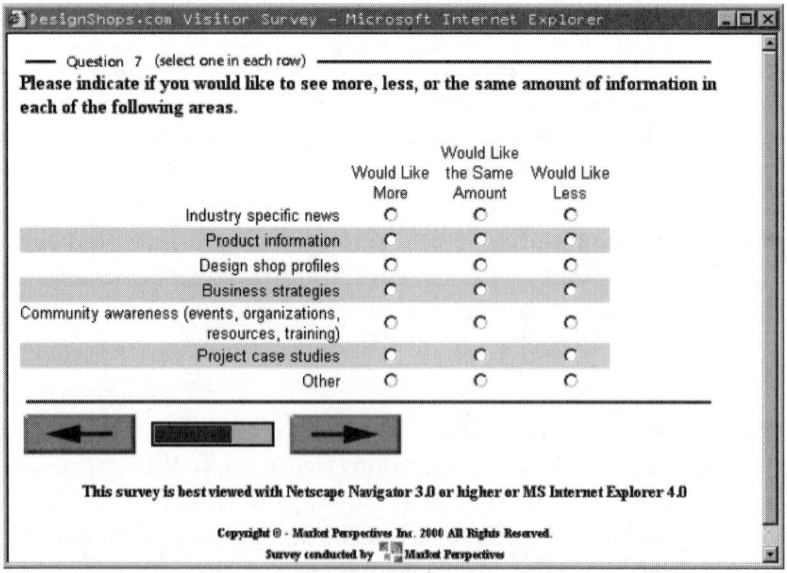

Figure 5.4   Question 7 in WebReview.com survey *(Reprinted with permission of CMP L.L.C, WebReview.com, Manhasset NY. All rights retained by CMP Media LLC.)*

Subsequent questions gather data about what sorts of information users want from the web site (Figure 5.4). This feedback will help the designers decide how much time and space to devote to each area; for example, areas that no group appears to be reading should be re-considered (either the information needs to be cut or it needs to be made more attractive or important to users). And notice the progress bar in the survey—a useful navigation feature. This lets users get a sense of where they are, more or less, in the survey. Without some sort of progress bar, or "page X of Y" indicator, users won't know if they have one question left or one hundred, making them more likely to quit before the end.

Survey Worksheet

On a separate sheet, generate a list of **categories of information** that you want to find out, and in each category, **specific things you need to discover.** This outline will eventually become your survey.	
Can the survey be anonymous? (Users are sometimes more likely to provide information if their identity will remain hidden, especially if they want to criticize—and remember that you **want** their criticism.)	
What do you want to tell users the purpose of your survey is? (Who benefits from the information? Why?)	
Can you offer some sort of reward to users for completing the survey?	
Go back to your list of specific information needs and decide what type of question or item will best address each: true or false, Likert scale, multiple choice, short answer, or other.	

(continued)

Can you use software to gather data? (For example, can you or someone else code a web page to gather the data automatically? Can you use some form of machine-readable sheet to gather large amounts of data?) Investigate the possibility of writing a program to run on your web server; you may be able to gather and analyze your data while the survey's being taken.	
Can you use software to analyze data? Statistics software (or even spreadsheets) can be invaluable in helping you figure out averages, trends, and so on, but if you don't plan on this use ahead of time, translating information into the program can be a burden.	
What different types of users do you have? Can you insert a question (or two) into the survey that will help you sort users into different types?	
Can you find users to beta test the survey for you (to make sure all questions are understandable, that enough space is provided for short answers, and so on)?	

Interviews and Focus Groups

Even if you gather very useful, general information from your survey, you may find that you need to work more intensively with one to five additional users (or more, depending on the scope of your project, your timeline, and your budget). A major endeavor like Microsoft's web site might be the result of tens of thousands of surveys over time and scores of in-depth interviews, focus groups, and usability studies.

In an interview, you'll work individually with a user or potential user to gather his or her insights, responses, concerns, and other information that will help you craft a useful, effective web site. In a focus group, you'll bring together a handful of users (three to five) and ask them to provide information in response to open-ended questions ("Would you use this web site?") or ask them to accomplish a specific task ("What are the top five worst things about this site?"). By asking people to hash out their ideas in a group, they'll often not only identify potential problems but also solutions. As people discuss the web site (and its pros and cons), they'll tend to not merely answer your direct questions but also engage in very exploratory and dynamic thinking, in some ways echoing the brainstorming processes that you work through as you develop the site. Unlike one-on-one interviews, people participating in focus groups are usually more than willing to express their opinions, offer advice and criticism, and explore new ideas.

On a separate sheet, generate a list of **categories of information** that you want to find out, and in each category, **specific things you need to discover**. This outline will eventually become your interview script.	
Can the survey be anonymous if you're going to share data with anyone else? (Users are sometimes more likely to provide information if their identity will remain hidden, especially if they want to criticize—and remember that you **want** their criticism.)	
What do you want to tell users the purpose of your survey is? (Who benefits from the information? Why?)	
Can you offer some sort of reward to users for completing the survey?	

(continued)

Go back to your list of specific information needs and decide how you'll frame each question or prompt. Remember that you should provide the opportunity for users to give you information. Don't ask yes or no or similar closed-ended questions.	
Sort your questions (within sections) from general to specific, but end each section and the overall interview with an open-ended, "Are there any related issues that you'd like to talk about?"	
Be sure to prompt users for concrete details if they're not giving them to you. ("That's interesting—can you tell me a little more, specifically, about that?" or "Can you give me an example?")	
Don't forget to thank your users for their help.	
Can you connect the interview process with other types of information gathering (for example, a short usability test)?	

Usability Testing

Usability testing and participatory design are actually very closely related: in traditional usability testing, designers will bring in selected prospective users to work with a product. While observing the person, the designers gather information about problems the client has with the product. For web sites, such testing typically involves asking a user to sit down with a web site and use it for a period of time.

To get effective usability testing results, you'll need to think carefully about several issues. First, what features of your site do you want to

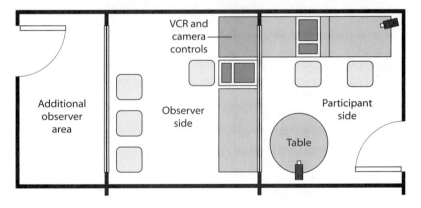

Figure 5.5   Sample usability lab configurations. Top: Clarkson University Video/ Usability Lab being used to videotape a user testing a web site. Bottom: Microsoft Usability Lab layout for large-scale usability testing. *(Screen shot reprinted by permission from Microsoft Corporation.)*

test? If you have a site of any size at all, you'll find that any particular user will see only very small slices of the site. (That's not a bad thing— it's the nature of a web site.) Second, you'll need to set up a task for your user to complete. There's nothing more confusing for a user to be taken out of his or her workplace or home, plopped in front of a computer, and under the scrutiny of professional designers, be told, "OK, start clicking." Instead, you'll need to situate your users in some familiar task. Think carefully, first, about who that user is supposed to represent in your audience. Is he or she a student visiting a department's web site in order to find out which courses will be offered next semester? This type of user would have a very different task from, say, a potential employer visiting a department's web site to see what types of courses a graduate student in the program would have taken. And both of these users are different from admissions boards of graduate programs, who might be looking at the web site to see if they're familiar with the research and publications done by faculty in that program.

What users will you invite? And do they represent your primary audience(s)?	
Where will you have them work? Will that area allow you to observe them without being intrusive?	
Do you have access to audiotaping or videotaping equipment?	
What tasks will you have them work on? (You can "mock up" tasks provided you think carefully about them. For example, "In this scenario, you're attempting to find out whom you need to call at our company in order to request information about our new line of widgets. Start at this screen, and go ahead and find the contact information you need.")	
What support materials will they need? (For example, can you give them a list of tasks to refer to? Or background information?)	

(continued)

After you've developed a list of tasks and support materials, translate that into a written script you can refer to—this will also help you keep each usability test consistent.	
Develop an introduction (welcome users, explain test procedures, reassure users that you're testing your web site, not their abilities, and that you expect to find problems). Add the introduction to the script.	
Consider also developing a brief exercise that asks the users to complete a task and verbalize what they're doing—some users need practice in verbalizing, and this practice may help.	
Develop a debriefing script. Ask for clarification of any issues, feedback on things they had problems with or liked, and so on.	

Participatory Observation and Design

As useful as traditional usability testing is for helping you see how real users interact with your web site, the method still lacks a good connection to your users' actual **contexts.** What users do in your usability lab or office may vary quite a bit from how they work on the job. For example, you may find that in your relatively quiet usability lab they have no problems reading five screens of information in order to resolve a question they have; in the workplace, however, they may face constant interruptions from ringing phones, questions from co-workers, and more. The web site you thought was a complete success after testing in your lab may be a total wash when it comes to real-world uses.

Two types of research can help you address those issues: participatory observation and participatory design.

Participatory observation involves watching your users interact with your web site within their own workplace (or wherever they would normally use your web site). With either a live web site or a version stored on a disk, you ask someone to use your web site in the context of a real job they're doing. If your web site offers clipart for small business publications, you'd ask the users to begin work on an actual publication they need, using your site as a resource. You would track their experiences—which screens they looked at, where they backtracked, how they downloaded files, how they placed them into their newsletters, and so forth. Occasionally, you might ask for clarifications or explanations ("You backed up to the previous screen—can you explain why?"). In most cases, you would have already completed traditional usability tests to make sure that the microlevel features of your site operated correctly (no pages were missing, steps were easy for users to follow, and the like). At the user's site, you're interested in how well your web site integrates with their own work processes. In this specific case, for example, you might find that the format you've stored your clipart images in conflicts with the software the user has (something that traditional usability testing might miss completely).

Participatory design comes in a step earlier, requiring you to watch your users at work for an extended period (hours, days, or weeks) to get a sense of their typical workflow. Only after gaining this experience do you begin thinking about the design of the site (and, in addition, involving the users directly in the process of design). By "shadowing" the user throughout the day, you attempt to understand what his or her work life is like, on both a micro- and macroscale. How might your web site better support that work? Your site may have an overall goal, but are there things you could be doing for this specific user to improve or add to your goal?

You might notice that as you look longer at particular users, as you gain more details about context, you run into a secondary concern: "What if I select a user who isn't representative of my whole audience?" This is certainly a very real concern—and one that's not easy to solve. That potential issue is exactly why you can't cover all of your bases with only one method—an effective web site design will require you to use multiple methods, constantly thinking about what your findings in each area say about the others as you progress. (This issue doesn't mean that you always have to use every available method—usually, you won't have time for that. But it does mean that you need to always be aware of benefits and limitations inherent in each method and be open to pursuing other methods as necessary.)

Gathering Information	
Would I benefit from getting in-depth information? How certain am I that the web site I'm developing will be useful to my users in their actual contexts?	
Can I identify any particular users who would both give me good information and have time to work with me?	
Can I isolate particular parts of a user's day to visit? Or will I miss important things?	
Could I ask users to keep a running, long-term log of their work in addition to or even in place of a physical visit by me?	
Will working with users give me crucial buy-in from my audience?	
Is the project important enough that I (or my company) can invest time in longer-term research?	
How am I going to record information (a notebook/tape recorder combination)?	
What specific things can I ask this user for assistance on? Are there areas that he or she can help me structure or rewrite?	

(continued)

Information Management	
How can I sort the information from the visit?	
What parts of my users' work or use could I better integrate into my design?	

Beta Testing and Post-Release Testing

In essence, beta testing means rolling out your site to a limited number of users and asking for their feedback (by email, phone, or other method). As users go through the site, they'll give you feedback about things ranging from broken links to confusing design or missing information. What specific information you gather is up to you. In some cases, beta testing will take place using a structure form on a web site that asks for feedback on specific items; in other cases (or sometimes in addition), you'll provide open-ended forms that allow users to insert any sort of comment or question.

Beta testing is a crucial step in web site development, particularly for large and very public sites. Even after extensive user testing, your final version of a site may have some unexpected problems. By beta testing the site, you essentially publish the site but give yourself a net in case you slipped up somewhere. The size of your beta test group is up to you. Some sites will even do a completely public (and publicized) beta test that is marketed in exactly the same way the final site is marketed; others may be as small as a handful of carefully selected users.

In addition, don't forget to post-release test your site. In other words, the journey isn't over just because you've published the site. Sites that are used by people often need frequent updates and periodic top-down revisions. You need to plan in methods for monitoring the ongoing use of your site (perhaps by integrating online surveys, as discussed earlier in this chapter). Other methods include follow-ups with users you may have identified earlier during usability tests or site visits, contacts with the client whom you completed the site for, leads that user groups provide you, simple mail-to text boxes on your site for feedback, and so on.

Are there things I can put on my site to generate feedback (mail-to forms, phone numbers, email addresses, and so on)?	
Will any of the users I identified earlier (during usability tests, for instance) be willing to provide ongoing feedback?	
Can I mail out surveys (to email lists, postal mail, office distributions, and the like) to bring new users in?	
Are there promotional materials that will be produced for the web site that might include requests for feedback?	
Can I reward users for feedback (perhaps randomly selecting one user for a $100 gift certificate)?	

Exercises

1. Go to the web site for a course you're enrolled in. If you were designing this web site, what methods might you choose for testing how usable the site is? Which two sample methods might work best? Which sampling method(s) might not work well? Which tests would you run and why?

2. In class, choose a web site that everyone in the class can usability test. As a class, develop three real-world tasks that users might complete at the site the class picked. Then, divide into four teams. Assign one team member to be the user while the other team members facilitate the usability test. Report the results to your class. Do they generally agree? If not, are there differences in the type of user in each team that might account for the differences? (For example, did one team have a relative computer novice, whereas another team had a senior computer science major?)

3. Assume you've been given the task of constructing a survey to improve customer satisfaction in your school's cafeteria. Construct a fifteen-question survey that will tell you what the top issues are. Then, construct a series of questions that a focus group could discuss to address the same topic.

As an in-class project, form a small role-playing group that will act as the focus group members. Assign the following roles for them to act out in the focus group: athlete, vegetarian, junk food junkie, and the homesick student who *really* misses Mom's cooking. Ask them to leave the classroom for a few minutes while the rest of the class constructs a schedule or list of topics and questions for the focus group to deal with. When the focus group returns, sit them at the front of the class and, with a class member or teacher moderating, ask them to address the topics and questions your class composed about cafeteria service. What sort of information was the focus group good at giving you? How well did the focus group turn out?

6 Structures: Organizing Sites

Objectives

- Seeing structure in action
- Understanding how different structures are used for different users and contexts

The structure of a web page or site provides users with important methods for understanding the material they're using. Structures provide both aids to understanding material and mechanisms for moving around in a site. In this book, when we talk about "structure," we're talking about the macrostructure of a web site—the relationships among different pages or nodes of a site—as well as the microstructure—the layout of particular pages. In this chapter, we'll discuss macrostructure; in Chapter 7, we'll cover microstructure.

Leslie, having finished her end-of-semester projects, decides to treat herself to a night out. She hasn't had time to catch any of the local bands, despite having picked which school to attend based on the local community nightlife. In one of her classes last week, two students on her web site design team spent most of the hour talking about the Spam Daggers show they saw at Zippy's Bar the previous Saturday. The band, apparently a local favorite for post-punkers, sounded exactly like what Leslie was looking for tonight. She accesses the web site for Zippy's Bar, and although it includes a calendar of shows, Leslie discovers that the Spam Daggers aren't playing at Zippy's tonight; another band she's never heard about, Whett, is playing. However, the previous week's calendar includes a link to the Daggers web site, so she clicks that.

The main page to the web site includes a brief biography of the band members (four of the six are apparently perpetual students), pictures, and a link to their show schedule. Leslie clicks that link, thinking, "Why wouldn't they put something important like where they're playing this week right on the main page?" She pulls up a long list of show dates, chronologically ordered. The Spam Daggers are apparently well known because they've been here **forever.** The list starts with play dates in 1994, scrolling off the bottom of the page. So Leslie scrolls and scrolls. 1994. 1995. 1996. 1997. "Forget it," she thinks, "I'll just go to Zippy's and take my chances with Whett."

Structure on ESPN's Web Site

On ESPN's web site, for example, designers attempt to address the needs of a diverse set of users. Some users come to the site with a particular goal in mind, such as finding the score for a recent sporting event. Other users may be interested in following a breaking story involving a particular athlete. Still other users may primarily wish to see "what's new"—in other words, read the site as if it were a newspaper, skimming across topics and occasionally reading the text of stories or viewing videoclips as they find intriguing topics.

In order to support this wide variety of users and contexts in mind, the designers of the ESPN web site have adopted a heavily gridded and compartmentalized interface, shown in Figure 6.1, that is the front end of a "hub-and-spoke" structure. Readers at the hub in Figure 6.1 click one of over 120 links (not including drop-down menus or text-entry boxes) to move outward from the main node. After reading information in the spokes, readers can return to the main hub to select a new spoke to follow. This hub-and-spoke structure, then, offers a way to deal with a diverse audience with different purposes or needs.

Users of the ESPN site can then move outward from this hub or main page to different spokes based on their own interests, such as the nodes shown in Figures 6.2 and 6.3 (pp. 64–65).

Figure 6.1   Main page for ESPN web site offering users more than 120 links
(*Courtesy of ESPN.com;* **REUTERS** ⬛)

In addition, the designers of the site have provided multiple structures to organize their site. Multiple structures are important for
managing large amounts of diverse types of information. For example, although we've described the site as having a hub-and-spoke
structure, the site also includes other structural devices, including:

1. Scrolling windows
2. Outlines
3. Radio buttons and standard buttons
4. Animation

Figure 6.2 ESPN site spoke on French Open *(Courtesy of ESPN.com;* **REUTERS** *)*

The outline structure, for example, occurs on the ESPN web site in two ways. First, in the box scores on the left, many of the categories (such as NBA) include links from both the main entry (NBA) and the subentries (Playoffs and Scores). Second, moving from page to page, users often gain incrementally more detailed discussions of the same general news item. In the move from the main hub to the spoke about the French Open, for example, users can select links to get additional information about the French Open. Users viewing the screen shown in Figure 6.2 can click a secondary spoke link to read additional information about Venus Williams's "easy third-round victory" (Figure 6.4, p. 66).

Figure 6.3   ESPN site spoke on soccer scores and schedules   *(Courtesy of ESPN.com.)*

Types of Structure

Although most printed texts contain a relatively simple structure (linear or outline with occasional cross-referencing), web-based texts and hypertexts generally adopt a much wider range of structures, often mixing multiple types of structures in a single site or even page. Therefore, the types of structures discussed here are only an introduction. Once you gain experience thinking about different types of structures and how they assist different sorts of users, you'll begin to see new types and hybrids, and perhaps even invent your own based on the particular users and context you're working with.

Figure 6.4   Secondary spoke on Venus Williams *(Courtesy of ESPN.com.)*

Each of these structures can be used in different situations, and any web site could adopt any one of these structures. Deciding which structure to use requires that you think carefully about the needs of your audience(s). Novices, for example, typically require a higher degree of structure or supporting framework, whereas experts often require much less. An expert often already possesses structural and relational information in his or her mind. For example, someone new to the concept HTML will normally need a slow, structured introduction that describes how tagging languages work, examples of codes with corresponding displays, and descriptions of classes of tags and the tags themselves. An expert, though, might only want to look up the syntax of a particular code (such as the options available in the <A HREF> tag). Supporting both users in a single site represents a tricky—but solvable—problem, provided each user's needs are carefully considered and appropriate structures are offered.

Linear (with Scrolling)

A linear structure with scrollbars offers probably the simplest structure for a web site: a single, long page. Although such sites were common in the early days of the Web, most users now find them difficult to read for a variety of reasons. For example, when users are two or three screens down in a single, long node, they may begin to lose track of where they are in the text. Unlike a printed book in which users can evaluate their progress by determining which page they're on (both in visual terms such as page numbers and physical terms such as how near they are to the front or back of the book), users of online texts frequently lack such cues.

For these reasons, among others, some web designers absolutely avoid any text long enough to require scrolling. However, for some situations, long nodes are suitable (Figure 6.5, p. 68). For example, users who are accustomed to reading long stretches of text may possess both higher degrees of motivation and better text-handling skills that will allow them to process such structures. In addition, because a well-designed web site should allow users to resize their browser window, in many cases the designer will have little control over whether or not a particular page requires scrolling. Finally, designers often will find they lack the time or support to do the additional work required to divide a long page into discrete nodes.

Linear (with Nodes)

Designers can also structure a linear site by linking a simple thread of nodes with forward and backward links that connect shorter nodes. Such a structure assists users in understanding their location within the site because sections are more clearly separated than they can be in a single, scrolling node (particularly if the designer also integrates page or section numbers on the individual nodes). Linear structures such as this are particularly useful when the designer needs to make sure that the user accesses material in a

Figure 6.5   Microsoft page with scrolling content *(Screen shot reprinted by permission from Microsoft Corporation.)*

particular sequence, such as a long block of text or a set of instructions. Figure 6.6 shows one node in a linear sequence from the Salon.com web site, which contains magazine articles longer than a typical screen. The "chunking" effect of the linear thread of nodes helps to break the information up into pieces small enough for users to manage more easily.

Outline

Outlines provide a classic structure for organizing material according to categories. Users are provided with a relatively small number of top-level choices that they can skim quickly. After choosing a top-level category, users can skim subcategories for increasingly detailed information. The outline gives users a filtering mechanism as well as an organizational structure. Outlines, therefore, are particu-

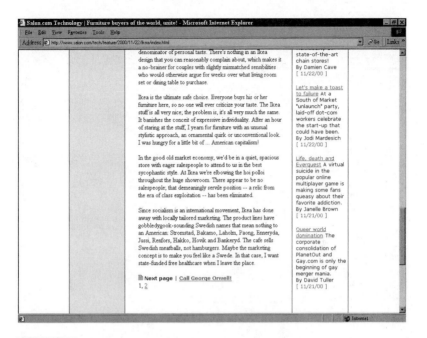

Figure 6.6   Scrolling and linked content in Salon.com article *(Reprinted with permission, Salon.com.)*

larly useful for users who are learning a large amount of new information or who need particular pieces of information from a very large site. Search engines, discussed later, are also often useful in these situations, provided the user is able to determine appropriate search terms to enter (Figure 6.7, p. 70).

Hub and Spoke

As discussed earlier, the hub-and-spoke structure can help designers handle users with very different goals or needs. Because the hub can contain a large number of choices, carefully designed hubs can allow users to quickly skim a main page and select a topic that interests them. As they move out to the spoke or subspoke pages, users read more detailed information. Subpage links back to the main hub allow users to browse a site, moving out to spokes and back as necessary, as shown at the Julie Davis site in Figure 6.8 (p. 71).

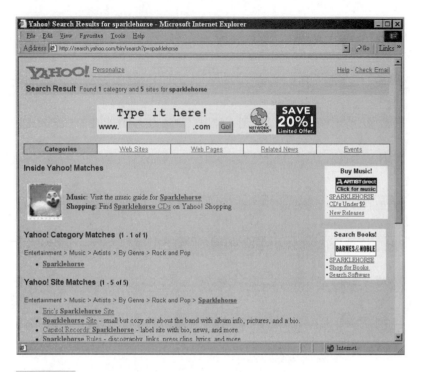

Figure 6.7   Search results page at Yahoo *(Reproduced with permission of Yahoo! Inc. © 2000 by Yahoo! Inc. YAHOO! and the YAHOO! logo are trademarks of Yahoo! Inc.)*

Partial Network

Networked sites allow users to move from node to node in a site with little regard to hierarchies or predictable structure. Frequently, networked sites offer connections from one node to another based on opportunistic association. Network structures work well when users may need to move across categories or when information—and user needs—do not require categories but, instead, work well with multiple and ad hoc connections. The structure of the World Wide Web is, in one sense, primarily a network, with users moving from node to node across different sites around the Internet. In most cases, partial network designs co-exist with other structures, providing users with different choices for navigation. In the MacInTouch web site in Figure 6.9, (p. 72), users can follow links from the main articles in the

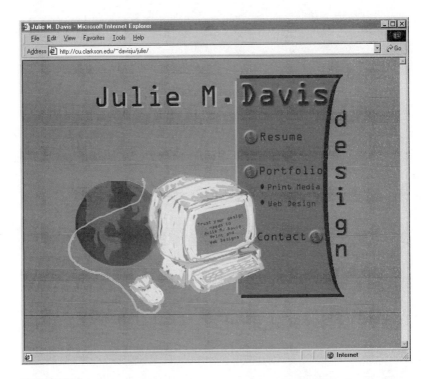

Figure 6.8   Hub and spoke structure (main page and "Web Design" secondary page) at designer's web site. *(Copyright © 2001 Julie Davis. All rights reserved.)*

middle column out to relevant external sites on the Web. Internal network-style links in the right column allow users to jump to recent stories. A navigation bar near the top of the screen provides limited outline structure, by allowing users to jump to one of six major categories on the site (some of those links subsequently become hub-and-spoke links, full network links, or other hybrid types).

Full Network

In some cases, the diversity of information contained in a site is best handled by letting users enter keywords into a search engine interface, then allowing them to move directly to a suitable node while they view the results of their list. Search engines, then, are something akin to a completely freeform network, with every node connected to

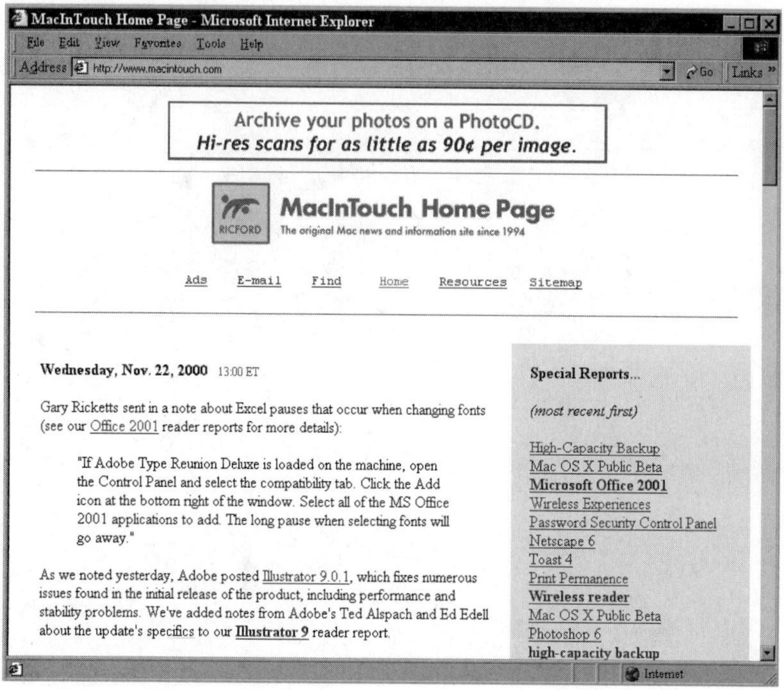

Figure 6.9   Partial network design on MacInTouch web site *(Copyright 1994–2001 by MacInTouch, Inc. All rights reserved. Reprinted with permission.)*

every other node on the fly. Search engine approaches are suitable for extremely large sites, especially those with expert users. Although it is possible to design sites for novice users, it is often difficult to index the site in a way that will allow novices to enter useful search terms. As with partial network designs, full network structures usually exist alongside another, less open structure. In Figure 6.10, users at the famously sparse Google.com search engine can search an index of web sites. The I'm Feeling Lucky button provides a search engine in which users type in a term and go directly to the first web site in their results list, bypassing the results pages used by most search engines.

Although most of us will not build massive, full-network sites like Google or Alta Vista, you should bear in mind that if you do include even a small search engine on your site, you need to think carefully about potential user paths. For example, if your primary structure is

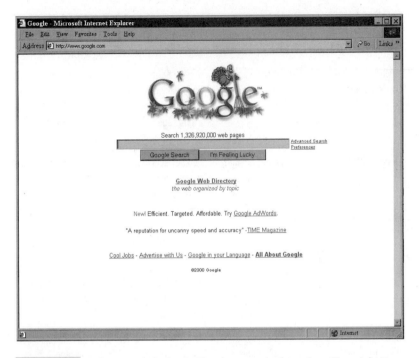

Figure 6.10   Full network design in Google.com search engine *(Copyright © 2000. Reprinted with permission of Google®, Inc.)*

a linear plus node approach, you may normally assume users have read nodes 1 and 2 in a story before reading node 3. However, a search engine may deliver users to node 3 without having read nodes 1 and 2. What methods can you use to get them to jump back to node 1? Furthermore, because most standard web sites will be indexed by one or more webwide search engines or indices, it's likely that users will arrive at subnodes in your web site even if you don't have a search engine on your site.

Design Sketches

As an aid to helping you think about how you might go about actually designing a web site, I've duplicated, in Figures 6.12–6.15 (pp. 76–81) some preliminary design sketches that walk you through the process of connecting user analysis to concrete designs.

Table of Structure Types

Structure Types	Description	Pros	Cons
Linear (with scrolling)	Users move up or down a long page by clicking on scrollbar	Very straightforward and familiar (like reading text down a long page)	Requires users to move in single line; easy for readers to lose their place on the page in very long nodes
Linear (with nodes)	Users move forward or backward in site by clicking sequential links	Simple navigation; reveals only one screen of information at a time (cuts down on amount of information in a single node)	Requires users to move in a single line
Outline	Users' access is increasingly detailed from lists of more general topics	Provides hierarchical structure to organize information	Hierarchical structure not always suitable
Hub and wheel	Users select one of many links to move outward from a main node	Allows single page to support very large number of uses	Can become information dense and confusing; prevents much depth on any single topic in hub page
Partial network	Users move in multiple directions, traversing a network	Allows users to move across a site based on multiple associations rather than strict hierarchy	Users can become lost in information space, unsure where they are in site
Full network	Users move to any node in a site by typing in keywords or search terms	Provides users a method for digging directly to useful information on a very large site	Users must know proper search terms

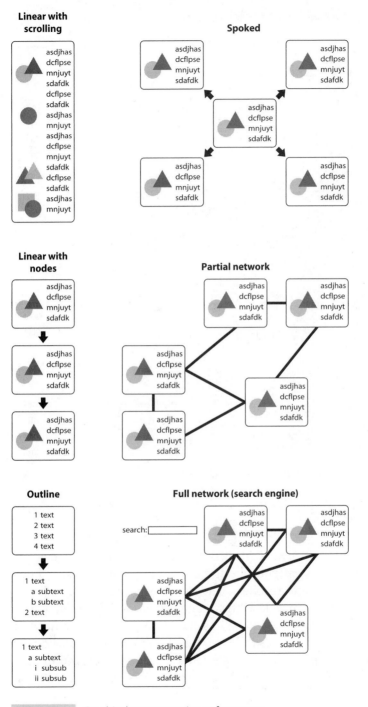

Figure 6.11 Graphical representations of structure

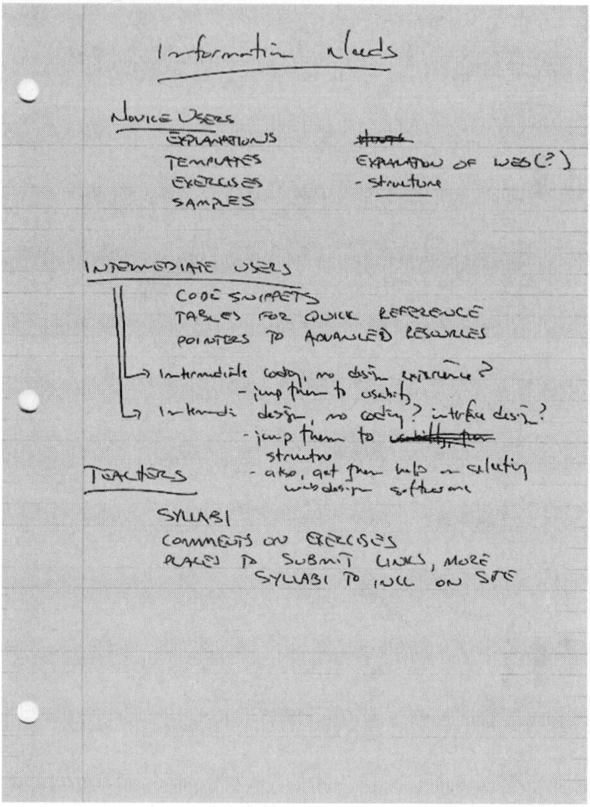

Figure 6.12 Information needs sketch

The initial sketches in Figure 6.12 deal with user information issues. This first page is designed around three groups: novice users, intermediate users, and teachers. The information in the three lists is based on extensive work with students in various classes at a number of universities; on feedback gathered from an early, partial draft of the manuscript reviewed by seven college professors who used web site design projects in their courses; and on background reading in web site design since the birth of the Web in the late 1980s. In the lists, I'm attempting to think through the types of information that each group will come to the web site for. Users new to web site design, for example, will require some structure to their learning; they may not yet know what issues are important or even how to start thinking about the design of a web site. For those reasons, the notes contain lists of information that are largely high level (explanations, structure, and so forth). Users new to the area you're covering in your web site will need some guidance: you need to help users construct categories, understand relationships, and become familiar with what they need to know.

The section on intermediate users, however, has a different order of information in it. Intermediate users, by definition, already possess a rough understanding of the area covered by the web site. They're not interested in introductory issues like "What is the Web?" Instead, they typically already have well-specified goals in mind and want to achieve them as quickly as possible. Note how the sketches prioritize quick movement—"Tables for Quick Reference," for example, will allow intermediate users to skim information more quickly and selectively than linear, paragraphed text.

Interestingly, part way through the sketch of intermediate users, I remind myself of an important distinction: "intermediate" (like "novice" and "expert") is a relative term. In this case, it's likely that some users of the web site will already have extensive HTML and low-level coding experience but no background in usability or rhetorical or contextual approaches to web site design. These users would become bored with introductions to HTML, navigation basics, or structure discussions. For these users, I'll have to provide a fast path to new information about usability. Another group of intermediate users, though, may have experience in thinking about usability issues based on experience in software interface design or writing. Such users may already have a good background in usability theories but need to move quickly to discussions of navigation and structure in web sites.

Finally, the sketch considers teachers who have adopted *Designing Effective Web Sites* for their courses. In some cases, those teachers

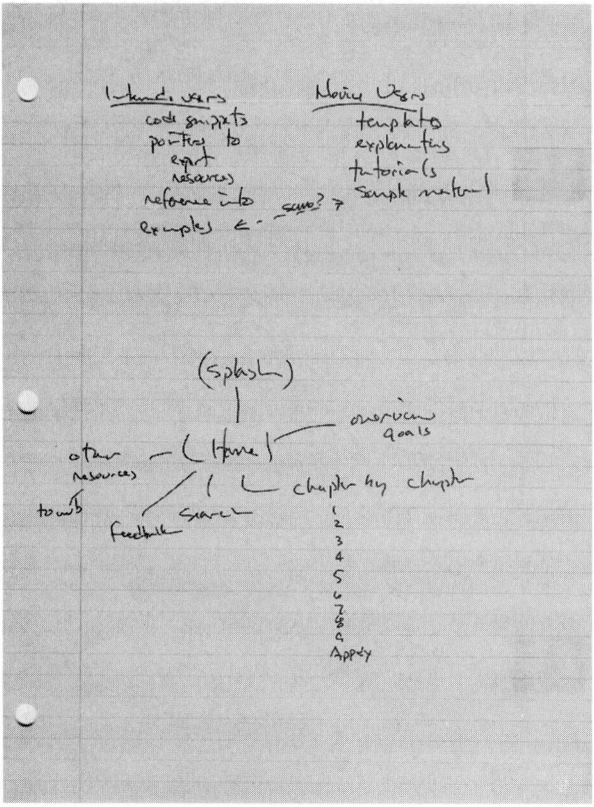

Figure 6.13 User's needs sketch

will be new to teaching web site design, so I need to provide sample syllabi (to help them structure their own courses). Other teachers may already have a good background in teaching web sites and just need explanations of exercises, additional resources, and an address to which they can submit new links and projects.

The second design sketch, in Figure 6.13, begins to apply that user analysis to a structural map of the site. At the top of the page, I begin to think how novices will approach the site. Because they don't already possess a firm understanding of the crucial issues, it's important to provide them with structure. Novices who don't have a structure in which to bring in new information frequently find themselves confused and frustrated. The book structure itself—the chapters and sections—are designed primarily for such users. The overall book begins with more general issues, then delves successively into deeper sections. Therefore, I've decided to arrange the primary structure for novice users around the sequence I designed for the book. Facilities for cross-linking are indicated, but not given primacy because (ideally) novice users will start with page one and move slowly through until the end, building their knowledge of design carefully and with strong foundations.

The section on intermediate users illustrates how they might approach the site in terms of its structure. These users may occasionally work from chapter outline, but in general, they'll have very specific goals in mind: assignments their teacher has made, snippets of code they can integrate into projects they're working with, and tools they might use to design web sites. Recall that intermediate users broke into two groups—those experienced with coding web pages but not thinking about users (who will require help finding worksheets and assignments) and those experienced with design but not web sites (who will need to quickly find help on software for web site development, among other things).

Figure 6.14 begins to bring together macrostructural (site navigation) and microstructural (screen layout) aspects for both novices and intermediate users. Because of the differing information needs and abilities of each group, the initial sketches in Figure 6.14 provide different sorts of material. Sketching out multiple structures for a site is a normal part of the process, indicating multiple audiences or users. At some point in designing the site, however, the designer will need to come up with a usable way to unite the two interfaces into a single, usable site and layout, one that works effectively for a range of users. In cases where the needs of user groups diverge to such a degree that they cannot be handled by a single interface or structure, the designer can decide to provide multiple subsites within a site for each group.

Finally, in Figure 6.15, the lists of user information needs and structural maps are converted into tentative interface screen designs. The

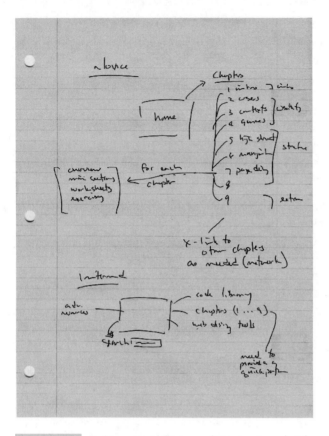

Figure 6.14   Early novice and intermediate structure sketch

key in this step is to remain open to design issues and multiple audiences. The most effective web sites need to provide multiple paths through the site for different users. At the top level, at least, the interface needs to deal with very different users in careful ways. By examining the earlier user and structure sketches, I've been able to establish that although intermediate users, novice users, and teachers may need different information, all of them can be oriented around the four primary topics structuring the textbook. Therefore, that element becomes a primary feature of the home page of the

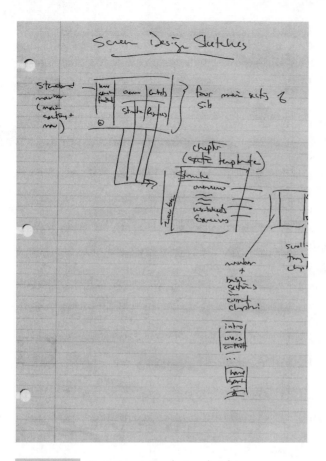

Figure 6.15   Tentative screen design sketches

site. From there, novices, intermediates, or experts can jump to information they need. If necessary, I can easily add subsection titles to each of the four sections.

Most sites, including this one, will encourage users to move around experimentally, so I intend to provide a standard navigation bar to give them an anchor point. Because frames work unevenly (especially for academic users, whose systems vary considerably), I've decided to structure the page as a table rather than a frame. The left column will contain a standard navigation bar to allow users to quickly access home, search, and related standard pages. (Although occasionally you can design a site without a navigation bar, in most cases, you'll want to include one because of the anchoring effect it has for users.)

Subpages in the sketch illustrate potential designs for pages for each chapter (because each chapter will contain a consistent interface, it was necessary to draw a rough sketch of only one). The chapter pages will include a fast track for intermediate users, who will need to jump directly to necessary sections in each chapter. Novice users, on the other hand, will be encouraged to scroll linearly through the chapter, at least on their first visit, in order to learn an overall structure for the material they're learning.

In order to help me think about the standard navigation bar in these chapter pages, I've sketched out some models. Although you don't always have to sketch things at this level of detail before beginning to work on a site, if special situations come up when you're thinking about a site, it's useful to jot down notes to remind yourself later.

As you can see from the notes, my ideas about content and design shifted at times during construction of the list of information needs, structure, and interface. This is normal—if you're able to sketch out a full, large web site without any rethinking in the whole process, you're probably oversimplifying the problem.

Bear in mind the nature of these sketches—they're quick, exploratory exercises. Use them to get you started and to begin brainstorming site features and functionality. Don't worry about correctness or neatness. (Obviously, I wasn't worried about little issues like handwriting legibility here.) The point is to help yourself think about the design work you'll soon be doing.

Structure Worksheet

Decisions about structure rely, in many cases, on your analysis of users. For that reason, many of the issues in your structure worksheet will be driven by a consideration of what your users want, need, or have to do. For example, designers of online libraries or similarly oriented sites begin by thinking about how their users will work with the information online. In many cases, users come to the site with two types of goals. First, some users will know a keyword or other term they want to use to narrow the full list of materials to a subset they can skim before selecting one or more elements for retrieval. These uses would obviously benefit from a search engine that lets them compile a list of likely resources they could retrieve. A second type of user will want to browse the site based on topic, author, or other category. These users will benefit from a structured, outline-oriented site that lets them select

Begin by listing the one to three primary groups of users who will visit your site.	
For each group, what specific pieces of information will they want to find or what goal will they wish to achieve?	
How will users be able to get to that information? In other words, can they specify exactly what information they want or topic they need, or will you have to help them with outlines or search tips?	
Refer to the table and graphic describing structure types on pages 74 and 75 to help you determine which structures will work best for your site. You'll likely need to adopt more than one structure to address multiple needs. (Or, in some cases, use one structure in one area of your site and another structure someplace else— let user needs drive your decisions.)	

progressively more detailed categories (for instance, biology, then subsets of biology, then perhaps resources on a specific species). It is important, then, that you let your answers to the worksheet questions be driven by careful thinking about your particular users. If you haven't already completed the user analysis worksheets, you may want to do that before undertaking the structure worksheet.

Exercises

1. Visit the web site for your school or some other organization you're affiliated with. Browse the site and think about the overall structure. Sketch out a map of the site on paper and decide which of the structure(s) in this chapter the site uses. Does it offer multiple structures? And if so, is one structure predominant?

   Randomly choose a different structure for the site and think about how that structure would change the site. Would users (or different types of users) find the site easier or harder to use?

2. Find a printed computer manual and use it to answer a question you have about using the software (for example, find a *User's Guide to Microsoft Word* and look up how to use the Track Changes tool to comment on another person's draft of a paper). As you work, record your movement through the structure of the print manual. What structure does the manual appear to have? If you're in a class, your teacher may assign related pieces of documentation (a user's manual, a quick reference card, a tutorial, an online help system) to different students or groups and ask you to compare structures.

3. Compose a question about national government that you would like to answer. The question can be as simple as "Who is my congressional representative?" or as complicated as "What is the relationship between the House and the Senate?" Visit a high-level government web site such as http://www.whitehouse.gov/ and attempt to find the answer to your question.

What is the structure of that web site? What types of users and information needs is it designed to support? Would a different structure provide you with a better experience? And would other users also benefit somehow from that structure? (Bear in mind that the "best" structure for many people would be a single node containing the exact information they were looking for. Unfortunately, most web sites have to support many types of users and masses of information, so structure is a negotiation between individual and group needs.)

7 Pathways: Elements of Navigation

Objectives

- Understanding what navigational devices are on web sites
- Choosing appropriate navigational devices for different types of users and contexts

Navigational Devices

In order to get from one node to another in a web site, you need to provide users with **navigational devices.** In general, these devices operate with roughly the same outcome—replace one set of information on screen with another set of information. In practice, precisely what devices you choose will depend on many factors, including the patterns you think users will read in, how many links you have between nodes, and how consistent your structure is. In many cases, you'll combine multiple navigational devices to deal with different users (or even different types of use from a single user).

Navigation in a web site is frequently a difficult problem because users have fewer contextual cues than when they use a print document. Turning a page in a print book invariably brings one to another page or, at the most, to the end of the book (in fact, few print navigation experiences are as jarring as **not** finding what one expects on turning a page).

This chapter helps you figure out what types of devices to use for which purposes. In addition, you'll see examples of different navigation devices in use. Finally, you'll experiment with different ways of setting up navigation devices in exercises provided at the end of the chapter.

Type of Device	Description	Pros	Cons
In-text link	Allows user to click on a specific word or page in a passage	Allows immediate movement while user reads a passage Simple to code	Links may not stand out to reader Sometimes difficult to cue reader to contents of target node ("Where does this take me to?") Sometimes difficult to come up with a good word for the link ("click here" syndrome)
Navigation bar	Single line or column of text containing numerous standard choices	Consistent approach helps orient readers Can stand out on a page in small amount of space (compared to button)	Requires relatively consistent structure
Frames	Embedded, static navigation bar (users click navigation bar to change content of other areas of screen)	Navigation frame remains fixed, providing users with anchoring point	Displays inconsistently in browsers Difficult for users to bookmark May break text-only browsers
Button	Graphical button on a page	Eye-catching (potentially) Suggests usage ("press")	Can take up a lot of space More time-intensive to produce Can require more computer memory

(continued)

Type of Device	Description	Pros	Cons
Search engine	Search field for entering random access searches	Quick access to anywhere in an indexed site	Can be more difficult to code
		Can allow access to huge amount of information	Users have to guess words to search on (may be a problem for novices)
Forward/backward, up/down, previous/next	Text or button allows users to move linearly in a text	Straightforward navigational pattern	Enforces linear navigation (fine in some cases, not in others)
Table of contents	Links outline-style table of contents to body text	Provides good structural organizer	Requires (or at least prioritizes) hierarchical organization
Automatic movement	Automatically move to a new node after set period	No user interaction required	No user interaction allowed
			Some users may become impatient

There are also combinations of these. A navigation bar, for example, can also include forward/backward buttons or be constructed out of a series of graphic buttons. In order to get a better sense of how these devices operate, let's look at some samples.

In-Text Link

An in-text link is one of the most common ways to allow users to navigate while they are reading text in a node. These work best for web sites with relatively free-form information and links because you don't have to come up with a consistent pattern (as with, for example, the navigation bar). When you want to provide a link to another node, you either select some text in the current node to link to the new one or write text describing what the next node holds. Research has shown that many users (especially on the World Wide Web) tend to only skim pages and may miss deeply embedded links, favoring bulleted lists, navigation bars, or buttons.

In the example in Figure 7.1, users click on the passage "Interesting things await us" to go to a new node in the text. In-text links such as this are most useful when you expect users to pay relatively close attention to the text on the screen. The in-text link allows them to find out about links to other nodes while they're reading. These links are

Figure 7.1   In-text link. Screen from Mark Bernstein's "The Limits of Structure." In-text link "Interesting things await us" links to new node *(Copyright © 1998 by Eastgate Systems, Inc. All Rights Reserved.)*

less suitable to web sites that will be skimmed by readers (who may completely miss the link or read only the text specifically designated as a link and therefore miss the full meaning). In such cases, you may want to either drop in-text links or supplement them with other types of links.

Navigation Bar

Navigation bars provide users with a relatively compact space for accessing standard sections in a web site. For example, a navigation bar might be used throughout a web site to allow users to jump to the top of one of five main sections in a site (overview, background, discussion, recommendations, appendices). The links are typically arranged horizontally in a row or vertically in a column to conserve space. These devices work best when they are used repeatedly— with the same links—in a site. If the links in a navigation bar change unexpectedly, users are more likely to be confused.

In Figure 7.2, designers of the Microsoft site (who must deal with literally millions of potential users with a seemingly infinite number of purposes) have provided a set of repeated navigation bars at the top of every screen in the site. The navigation bars serve to divide the site up into manageable sections for users, and allow users to jump to the top of one of the main sections or areas with a single click no matter where they are in the site. Such navigation devices rely on the designer's ability (and the user's need) to think of the web site in large sections or functions.

Frames

Frames lead an embattled existence: designers seem to either love them or hate them. In most cases, frames are methods for dividing up a browser window in order to allow each separate area of the window to change independently of the others. In terms of navigation, frames allow designers to insert a fixed navigation bar or pane that remains in place while other sections of the window change. (In essence, button bars in browsers like Netscape Navigator and Internet Explorer are fixed frames offering back and next buttons.) The web site in Figure 7.3 includes frames, including a vertical "Kairos

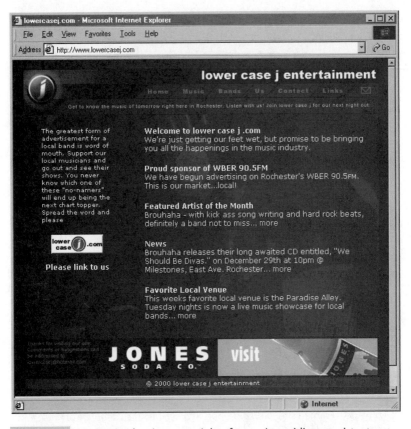

Figure 7.2 Navigation bar (near top right of screen) providing consistent controls for movement within the site. *(Copyright © 2001 Matt Stoffel. All rights reserved.)*

5:2" frame in the leftmost column that allows users to jump back to the main web site. In addition, the article itself includes a vertical navigation frame, with "Introduction," "Research," and other buttons. As users navigate the site, the content of some frames remains the same while the content of other frames changes. For example, users who scroll down the middle frame (titled "Introduction") will see changing content while the other frames remain unchanged, providing mental stabilizers.

At first glance, frames seem like an obvious solution to the problem of navigation bars that can disorient readers by disappearing and

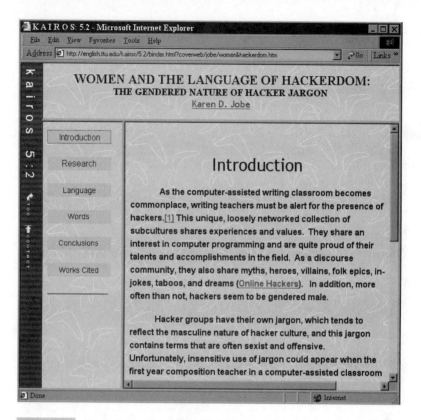

Figure 7.3   Framed site *(Karen D. Jobe, "Women and the Language of Hacker-dom: The Gendered Nature of Hacker Jargon." Reprinted with permission of the author; Reprinted with permission.)*

then reappearing with each click: users have a fixed point of reference to help them from becoming lost within a large and complex site. However, frames have several drawbacks that require very careful thought and coding as well as user testing for success. First, frames require designers to code each area or "pane" of the screen as a relatively independent file. Some WYSIWYG browsers assist designers by coordinating the files on screen automatically and managing the separate files in the background—but in the end, designers are still working with multiple files on each screen when they use frames. Second, and perhaps most important, frames can cause users difficulty in bookmarking and printing screens (because most browsers apply bookmarks and printing commands to only one of the frames present in a screen). Third, users relying on text browsers such as Lynx will have difficulty understanding the layout of the page. Fourth, frames display inconsistently from one browser to another, making it difficult to precisely control page layout. Finally, because each area in a multiple-frame window exists on the web server as a discrete file, search engines that index a site will reference (and then display to users) only individual frames, not the full and laid out arrangement of frames the designer composed.

Do these drawbacks mean you should never use frames? No, frames can be an excellent resource for addressing complicated navigation and structure problems. Talented and careful designers can deal with all these issues through techniques such as multiple versions of a page keyed to different browsers or for printing, careful use of META tags (hidden tags containing additional information about a page) to assist search engines, and extra coding to detect when a browser loads only a single frame (to force the browser to reload the whole framed page).

Button

Buttons, like in-text links, work best for links that are created individually (as opposed to structural elements in a navigation bar or previous/next links). Buttons are traditionally more "graphical" than text and are often used to catch the user's eye and suggest action (pushing the button). In the example in Figure 7.4 (p. 94), visitors to Purdue University's web site can click one of many buttons to jump immediately to the top of a section. Buttons tend to take up more space on screen than text although careful designers can often design legible small buttons if necessary. In addition, the division between "text" and "button" exists more in practice than in principle: if the design suggests to the user that the link is a button, it's a button.

Buttons are useful because they attract attention and suggest a straightforward action: the push of a button. As such, they are useful when you want to offer users a limited number of options. Although buttons can be supplemented with other navigation devices, their nature causes many users to consider them the primary method for navigation.

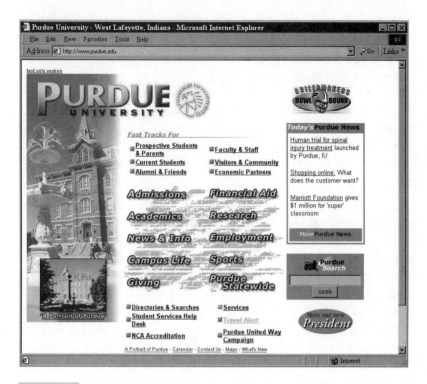

Figure 7.4 Buttons on a page link users from main page to subsections
(*Reprinted with permission.*)

Search Engine

Search engines provide users with a way to freeform search a large or very complex site by typing terms into a form. Search engines can vary in their own complexity, from simple term searches (where users type in one or two terms to search for with no other capabilities) to very complex searches (where users enter Boolean operators, timespan delimiters, media types, and so on). Search engines are generally not as useful for small web sites, particularly when there are other methods for informing users about the overall structure and contents of the text. In addition, search engines often require that users already know an appropriate search term.

In the screen in Figure 7.5, from the web developers' resource Web-monkey, users have the option of typing in a search term to locate

Figure 7.5   Internal search engine in a site   *(Reprinted by permission; Copyright © 2001 Lycos Inc. All rights reserved.)*

pages in the site. Search engines are particularly useful in sites such as this because they store large amounts of information that users can jump to quickly. Typing in a term such as "navigation" will give users a list of resources for learning about navigation techniques at the popular Webmonkey site. Novice users, however, will often not know the appropriate term to search on, so alternative browsing methods should also be used. In the Webmonkey site, users can also skim a table of contents in the left column or read abstracts of recent entries on the main screen.

Forward/Backward, Up/Down, Previous/Next

Linear navigational devices such as forward and backward buttons help users move through a web site that has a relatively simple structure, much as the pagination of a print book allows readers to

I'm instantly your biggest fan. Historien · Personerna · Diskografi · Bilder · Multimedia · Tour · Press · Texter · Nyheter · Fanclub · Kuriosa ...
URL: home6.swipnet.se/~w-65679/radiohead/index.htm
Directory Match: Radiohead Fan Dedications
More pages from this site   Related pages

8. DATALOSS
UPDATED 10.2.2000 best viewed on netscape © 2000 **RADIOHEAD**/W.A.S.T.E./INCHING DEADWARD. ...
URL: www.radiohead.com/00.html
Translate   More pages from this site   Related pages

9. Radiohead?(Neutraal)
Popmuziek Vraag & Aanbod Re: Wie speelt er op Pinkpop? (Neil Harmsen) Re: DIT KOMT ZEKER OP PINKPOP: (Roel Determeijer) Vorige:
is dat niet al...
URL: www.dds.nl/~cjp/SLOT/HN_MARKT/get.cgi/pop/7/4/9.html
More pages from this site   Related pages

10. Radiohead.org
A site dedicated to the British musicians known as **Radiohead**. News updated daily, contests and polls every few months....
URL: www.radiohead.org/
Translate   More pages from this site   Related pages

Result Pages: **1** 2 3 4 5 6 7 8 9 10 11 12 13 14 15 16 17 18 19 20   [Next >>]
word count: radiohead: 148756

Extend Your Search:

Shop the web for **radiohead**
Shopping? Compare prices from around the web on **radiohead** at mySimon
Find Yellow Page listings for **radiohead** at WorldPages.com
Shop best prices on **radiohead** or almost anything at DealTime!
Find **radiohead** and millions of other cool items at eBay!
Refine your search on **radiohead** with LookSmart Categories
· Get further insight on **radiohead** at MyPrimeTime
· Looking for audio/MP3 downloads? Search for radiohead in **Audio/MP3**

Figure 7.6   Embedded navigation bar with Next button on AltaVista® search
results page   *(Copyright © 2000 AltaVista® Company. All Rights Reserved.)*

move forward and backward in the document. This device is less
useful in complexly structured information because users will often
want to move in many different directions based on the different
structures in the document and on their changing needs.

Previous/next links are often used in online books (where users often want to move linearly through a succession of nodes) or other
long texts and in search engines, where the results of a search might
return hundreds or even thousands of entries. Because users of online texts tend to become lost more frequently than users of print
texts, long lists normally have to be broken down into manageable
chunks. In the Alta Vista search results screen shown in Figure 7.6, a
very long list has been broken down into chunks of twenty-five en-

tries each. Users move forward and backward through the long list of entries twenty-five at a time by clicking forward and backward buttons. Forward and backward buttons can be coded manually as simple links or as JavaScript items.

Table of Contents

Table of contents entries in web sites operate similarly to the familiar tables of contents in print texts: they provide users with a quickly scannable, hierarchical structure and allow them to jump directly to the relevant section of the web site. Essentially, the table is a topical list organized according to some scheme (level of difficulty, content area, and the like). Entries can be embedded, providing several levels in a hierarchical structure. Indexes are a special form of tables organized alphabetically. Because tables of contents imply (and in some sense require) a hierarchical or at least linear organization, they are not suited to web sites that use a heavily networked structure. In the Grad Staff and Fellowship Audit web site at Purdue University (Figure 7.7, p. 98), for example, a table of contents lists major sections and subsections of the site that users can quickly skim in order to find material they're looking for. The use of first- and second-level entries helps users locate material because they can skim first for high-level sections they need and then search that section for the more detailed entry. In addition, a well-designed table of contents can also educate users because it provides them with a highly structured overview of an area (much as the tables of contents are supposed to function in textbooks). Designers of tables of contents need to be sure that this organization will be helpful for a user (as opposed to, for example, a bulleted list or a series of question and answers to common issues).

Automatic Movement

Automatic navigation is considered less common in hypertext because it takes control of navigation away from the user by replacing one node automatically with another (usually based on time). Splash pages in many sites show users an initial page designed for some particular purpose (often the promotion of brand-name

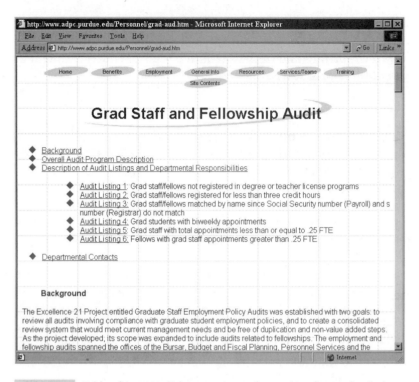

Figure 7.7　Table of contents links connect to other nodes of more detailed text *(Reprinted with permission.)*

recognition), which is then replaced by a subsequent main page. Time-based media—such as video, audio, and gif animation—are a special case of automatic navigation (where one image or sound is replaced by another in fairly rapid succession). In the Creating Killer Web Sites screens in Figure 7.8, users are greeted with an initial splash page that mimics the cover of the book (to which the web site is a companion). The splash page creates an initial impression but does not contain a great deal of functional information; after five or so seconds, the splash page is replaced by the main functional page of the site. Automatic navigation is useful in places such as this, where the designer wants to structure a user's experience over time. In this sort of automatic navigation, designers become more like film, television, or radio producers because they take responsibility

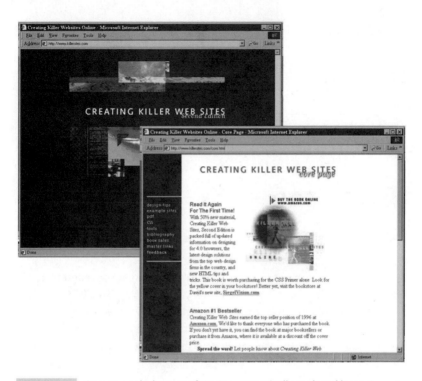

Figure 7.8   Opening splash page of site is automatically replaced by main page after several-second delay *(Courtesy David Siegel.)*

not merely for structuring the information but also for making decisions about how the work is displayed over time. CD-ROM games such as Myst represent a hybrid medium that is, in many ways, an interactive web site but, in others, a movie because from time to time users' actions will initiate automated sequences that play out as on-screen movies or narratives.

Navigation Device Decisions

Deciding which navigation devices to use in a web site requires that you think about the different ways that your users might want to move between nodes. Much of this decision should be based on the structure you're using in the web site (discussed in Chapter 6).

User Movement	Possible Devices
Linear	Previous/next (can be buttons or navigation bar)
Nonlinear (across network structure)	In-text links (written as necessary), possibly search engine
Random	Search engine
Up and down hierarchy	Table of contents, navigation bar, frame

Exercises

1. Go to the main page for your school, department, or program. What navigation devices can you find?

2. Find a site that provides information about a career you're interested in (use a search engine like http://www.yahoo.com or http://www.hotbot.com if you're not familiar with one). What would happen if you replaced one type of navigation device with a different type? Would the site be as usable? Are there navigation devices that just wouldn't work for that site?

3. Compete with your classmates on finding one web page that has the most different types of navigation devices on it.

4. Select a relatively long print-based document (novel, manual, catalog) and analyze the navigation devices used in it. If you're stumped, ask yourself how users of that document get from node to node in the document. If that document were online, what other navigation devices might you be able to offer to users to make the document more effective or efficient?

5. Can you think of cases where a print document would be easier to use than an online document? Think not only of document types but, especially, about contexts for use and purposes for using documents.

6. Can you think of (or find examples of) navigation devices other than those covered here?

Projects

1. Developing a Prototype

Assume you're developing the navigation system for a large phone directory for your company that will be used both internally and externally. Internal users will often know a person's name, but they may know just the division title or job responsibility, or even just the office address. External users may know only which product they're interested in or have a complaint about service or product quality. The directory will be based on a database that will hold several thousand entries. What navigation devices will you use? Why? Do you need additional information in order to make your choices (or to make more informed choices)?

2. Navigating Hypertext Fiction

Take the text of a short story and import it into a web site– or hypertext-authoring program. Break it up into small chunks (1–100 words) with one chunk per node. Experiment with different types of navigation devices and analyze how they affect reading. If you're in a class, you might divide into teams and, with each team using the same chunks of text, experiment with a different type of navigation device.

3. Revising Navigation in a Site

Find a site that you feel has poor navigation features. Revise the site (either on paper or online) for better navigation. What sorts of problems did you solve? What problems are still present and not easily solvable?

8 Layouts: Formatting Pages

Objectives

- Seeing page structure and layout in action

- Setting up grids for screens

U sers of web sites rely heavily on visual and logical structure as they work with a site. Unlike many linear texts, web sites usually assume that the text is a structure that can be navigated in different ways by different users. (See Chapter 6 for discussions of various types of structures.) Although structure is certainly important in many types of texts (particularly technical texts like computer manuals), web sites take the need for careful structure to new levels.

What would a web site be without structure? Consider the in-screen and between-screen navigation elements that are part of the Farm Club web site, a companion web site to a popular music television show (Figure 8.1).

Users coming to the web site obviously don't begin by reading every single word on this splash page, then following each link in order (in our culture, that would mean top left to bottom right). Instead, the Farm Club web site, like most effective web sites, offers users hierarchies of importance on the page. In other words, the designers have made some aspects of the page more prominent than others, inviting readers to find the section of the site that most interests them.

To take our Farm Club example, consider what the page would look like if the designers had taken out most structuring devices:

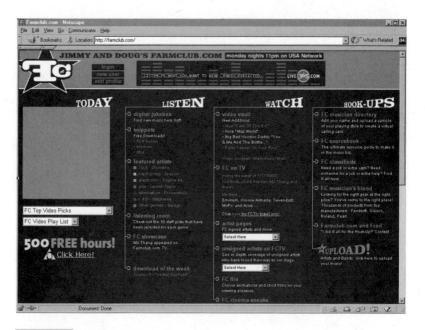

Figure 8.1 Farmclub.com web site *(Screen shots provided courtesy of Farmclub.com.)*

FC

Jimmy and Doug's Farmclub.com

monday nights 11pm on USA Network

login

new user

edit profile

listen to what you want to hear

radio perfected

live365.com

today

listen

digital jukebox

find new music here first

snippets

free download

ruff ryders

eminem

mya

featured artists

rock – chimera

rap/hip hop – DraCon

electronic – Empire 44

pop – Lauren Taylor

alternative – Flickerstick

r & b – Stephanie

other genres – Benign

listening room

check out the 10 staff picks that have been selected for each genre

FC showcase

Mz Thang appeared on Farmclub.com TC

download of the week

Jurassic 5 – "Verbal Gunfight"

This list is only the first two columns—around 30 percent—of the main page. Imagine how difficult it would be for users to skim the main sections of this page in order to use it. Most would give up.

In the screenshot in Figure 8.1, users will typically skim the screen quickly to find the main heading:

■ Farm Club splash page banner

and four major sections of interest on the site:

■ Today
■ Listen

- Watch
- Hook-ups

Not coincidentally, these main sections are made prominent through several design techniques:

- Size
- Location
- Color

Because the Web comprises millions of interconnected sites, it's crucial—especially on the main page of your site—to make sure that users can identify where they are. (For related reasons, it's also crucial that subpages look related to the main page of your site so that users know they haven't somehow wandered out of the site by accident.) Because of reading patterns in North American (and related) cultures, most readers will begin at the top of the screen where, as with most web sites, the designers have placed a large graphical banner containing the name of the site and other relevant information. Material that's placed lower on the page is also usually read later (if at all): users who are careful to also scroll down the page (probably a minority) will see four additional sections:

- Vote
- News
- Network
- Talk

Although in theory these four subsections are of equal importance to the first four (Today, Listen, Watch, Hook-ups), functionally they are subordinated because they are farther down the page (and, in many cases, won't even by seen by users who may find something of interest before they realized they can scroll down).

The designers have then divided the site up into (at least) four main sections and labeled those sections with the second most prominent visual element of the site: large, contrasting graphical headings along four vertical columns (Figure 8.2). Readers can skim to the right across this row of headings, dipping down into the subelements of each column if necessary in order to see if they're

Figure 8.2 Detail from Farmclub.com web site *(Screen shots provided courtesy of Farmclub.com.)*

interested in reading more detailed information. (The columns are typical "grid" elements in screen design, which we discuss later.) The hierarchical arrangement means that users can quickly scan all four headings, then come back to one for further reading.

Notice that the designers have recursively subdivided each of the four subsections of the site in hierarchical ways: The Listen section, for example, is broken into six subsections (Figure 8.3):

- ◼ Digital jukebox
- ◼ Snippets
- ◼ Featured artists
- ◼ Listening room
- ◼ FC showcase
- ◼ Download of the week

Users can click each of the subsection heads in order to pull up a new screen with additional material. In some cases, such as Featured Artists, users can also make selections one additional level deeper by clicking one of the artist's names in that section to call up additional material.

In addition to design elements such as size and color, effective web sites rely heavily on a screen layout in order to help users skim a page and understand how information is grouped together. In the Farm Club page, for example, we've already seen how readers locate the primary elements according to their visual size and location (vertical and horizontal) on the page. In addition, the designers have also "grouped" related information according to importance, laying out related items within visual chunks. They have also attempted to lay out elements that function similarly—such as the main subsections of the site—in logically and visually similar ways.

At the broadest level, the page is "gridded." Grids are crucial to nearly any document in which readers must understand structure as they

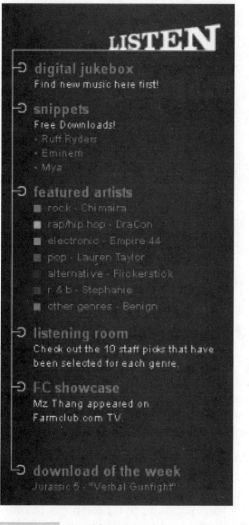

Figure 8.3   Detail from Farmclub.com web site *(Screen shots provided courtesy of Farmclub.com.)*

read and use the text; grids are a standard design technique developed for print texts such as newspapers. The Farm Club page, like most web sites, has a relatively simple grid, as shown in Figure 8.4.

As you can see from the overlaid grid, the designers have structured the page through a series of vertical and horizontal lines. Elements are then placed into the grid so that they fill either a square or a

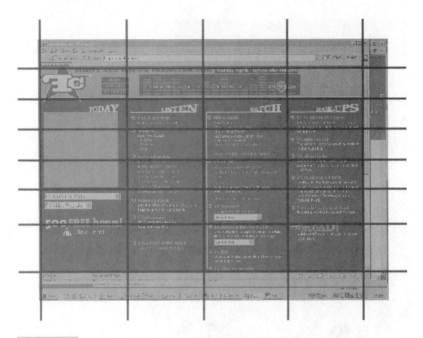

Figure 8.4 Grid overlaid on Farmclub.com web site *(Screen shots provided courtesy of Farmclub.com.)*

series of adjacent squares. The splash page banner takes up a horizontal series of four rectangles, spreading across the top of the first page. From a visual and logical perspective, the horizontal banner then acts to unite (and organize) the four vertical columns below it.

In most cases, you can't simply put elements wherever you want on a page when you design it. Common web languages such as HTML look at pages as if the information should be simply "flowed" down a page, left to right and then top to bottom. To lay out pages in rows and columns in a common grid pattern, you'll need to structure the page using an HTML table—one in which the lines dividing the rows and columns are made invisible. Another, more complex, option involves the use of frames (although Chapter 7 on navigational features discusses problems with using frames). See the Appendix on additional resources for information on designing with HTML tables and for pointers to more advanced design topics. And don't be afraid to experiment with your web site design software!

Figure 8.5   Major sections of layout from grid *(Screen shots provided courtesy of Farmclub.com.)*

Each of the four columns is relatively equal in width, with information running down each column. From a visual and logical perspective, the designers have used the grid to construct an array of five major areas of the page (Figure 8.5).

Information within these grids, then, is clustered according to relevance and category. The top banner is situated across the four subsection columns. The similarity of each column suggests to users that the material in each column is somehow related. (Keep in mind that these rules can be violated once they are understood. A designer could insert a vertical navigation bar across the left column, using color or other graphical techniques to override the suggested similarities to the other three content columns on the page.) By applying consistent gridding and clustering techniques to construct a visual and logical hierarchy to your page, you'll help your users understand how information is arranged on your page and in your site.

Web site users tend to have a zigzagging pattern, from higher to lower levels of importance. They begin by skimming at the top visual or logical levels of importance across a screen, dropping down successive levels as they find information that interests them. Without elements such as grids and clusters, users will have a difficult time skimming a screen—and using the site.

Exercises

1. Make photocopies (reducing if necessary) of two different print documents and use a colored pen to draw the grid used on each. What is the smallest grid space or rectangle? Have the designers combined grid rectangles (horizontally or vertically) in order to make larger elements? Have the designers used similar grid arrangements for similar clusters of items?

2. Search on the web for pages that don't rely very heavily on grids for layout (for example, pages with long, scrolling texts). What types of users would use these pages? Would a grid be helpful here?

3. Print out a web page from a site you use frequently. Identify the grid being used for the site and the major sections filling the grid. Then, come up with a new grid and sketch out a new version of the page. (As a class exercise, your teacher may ask each person in the class to redesign the same page so that you can compare results.)

Appendix

Additional Resources

Designing Effective Web Sites is only a starting point, a way to help you learn the principles and methods of creating web sites that are actually useful to people. I expect that as you learn the design principles covered here, you'll also begin learning from additional resources. For example, we haven't discussed software for creating web sites or HTML codes. As I explained in the introductory chapter, a growing and diverse set of packages support web site design—choose the one that fits your needs and budget; if you're working in a simple text editor (or if the manuals that came with your software aren't adequate), use one of the tutorials or reference guides for assistance. In addition, as you begin designing more advanced sites, you'll probably want to explore some of the professional-level resources on issues like graphic design, usability testing, and more. Web site design is a constantly changing profession—these resources will help you keep pace.

Straightforward HTML Guides		
Introduction to HTML and URLs	Thorough HTML and web tutorial (but lengthy)	\<http://www.utoronto.ca/webdocs/HTMLdocs/ NewHTML/intro.html\>
NCSA's HTML Guide	The original	\<http://www.ncsa.uiuc.edu/General/Internet/ WWW/HTMLPrimer.html\>
Barebones Guide to HTML	In numerous formats and languages	\<http://werbach.com/barebones\>
W3C HTML Home Page	The official HTML specifications	\<http://www.utoronto.ca/webdocs/HTMLdocs/ NewHTML/intro.html\>

Tutorials and Lessons (Coding, Design)

Webmonkey	Wired's massive coding and design tutorial and discussion resource	<http://www.webmonkey.com>
Yale Style Guide	Widely used reference on web design (focuses on structures)	<http://info.med.yale.edu/caim/manual>
Web Style Guide	Print version of Yale Style Guide (focuses on structures)	Lynch, Patrick J., & Horton, Sarah. (1999). *Web Style Guide*. New Haven, CT: Yale University Press.
HTMLCenter	News, reviews, tutorials, and tips on HTML and related issues	<http://www.htmlcenter.com>
Training Tools	Tutorials on wide range of web site design software	<http://www.trainingtools.com>
Getting Started with HTML	Excellent tutorial from the HTML governing body	<http://www.w3.org/MarkUp/Guide>
iBoost HTML site	Large, diverse set of HTML tutorials	<http://www.iboost.com/build/programming/html/index.html>

Commercial Software, Shareware, and Freeware

Macromedia Dreamweaver	Predominant choice among professionals (Mac+ Windows versions)	<http://www.macromedia.com/software/dreamweaver>
Microsoft FrontPage	The Redmond giant's popular web site program (Windows—Mac version outdated and buggy)	<http://www.microsoft.com/frontpage>
Microsoft Visio (Professional Edition)	Advanced flowcharting software for mapping site structures, storyboards	<http://www.microsoft.com/office/visio/professional.htm>
cnet's Five under $50	Review of website authoring programs under $50 (Windows)	<http://www.builder.com/Reviews/CheapEditors/?tag=st.bl.3881.edt.bl_CheapEditors>
BBEdit	Popular text editor for Macs— free and commercial versions	<http://www.barebones.com>
1st Site	Free Windows-based HTML text editor	<http://www.evrsoft.com>

Graphic Design Resources

DesignShops	Discussion of professional web site design (ranging from practical to managerial)	<http://www.designshops.com>
Design and Publishing Center	Portal for graphics designers	<http://www.graphic-design.com>
Design Bookshelf	Bibliography of print resources for graphic designers	<http://www.design-bookshelf.com>
Designing Web Graphics. 2	Advanced techniques for Web graphics design	Weinman, Lynda. *Designing Web Graphics: How to Prepare Images and Media for the Web.* Indianapolis: New Riders Publishing. (1997).
Creative HTML Design	Hands-on tutorial for web site design	Weinman, Lynda, & Weinman, William. *Creative HTML Design.* (1998). Indianapolis: New Riders Publishing. (See also, <http://www.htmlbook.com>.)
Xine's Web Resources	Extensive set of web resources for designers	<http://www.lightlink.com/xine/graphics.html>

Miscellaneous Resources

Dreamweaver Depot	Third-party Dreamweaver plug-ins, resources	<http://people.netscape.com/andreww/dreamweaver>
Bobby	Test web sites for ease of access by users with disabilities	<http://www.cast.org/bobby>
DrHTML	Checks spelling, links, and more on web pages	<http://www2.imagiware.com/RxHTML>
Secrets of Successful Web Sites	Case studies of successful web sites	Siegel, David. (1997). *Secrets of Successful Web Sites.* Indianapolis: New Riders Publishing. (See also, <http://www.secretsites.com>).
cnet's Website Authoring Pages	Massive set of tips, reviews, tutorials, and resources on wide array of programs (Dreamweaver, FrontPage, HomeSite)	<http://home.cnet.com/webbuilding/0-3881.html?tag=st.cn.7297-ron.bc.gp>
Writing for the Web	Good resource for text-level issues (style, sentence structure, clarity)	(print) Killian, Crawford. (1999). *Writing for the Web.* Bellingham, WA: Self-Counsel Press.

WebReview Magazine	Online magazine for web site designers	<http://webreview.com>
WebTechniques Magazine	Online and print magazine for web site designers, programmers, and system administrators	<http://webtechniques.com>
The Columbia Guide to Online Style	Standard reference on online style (particularly citation formats)	Walker, Janice R., & Taylor, Todd. (1998). *The Columbia Guide to Online Style.* New York: Columbia University Press.
Collaborative Web Development	(print) Theories and practices for working in web site development teams	Burdman, Jessica. (1999). *Collaborative Web Development: Strategies and Best Practices for Web Teams.* New York: Addison-Wesley.

Usability Resources

Jakob Neilsen's UseIt.com	Usability research and advice from the Web's most famous usability guru	<http://www.useit.com>
Designing Large-Scale Websites	(print) Good discussion of design processes and issues for large web sites	Sano, Darrell. (1996). *Designing Large-Scale Websites.* New York: John Wiley & Sons.
Designing Web-Based Training	Methods for setting up educational sites (learning, testing purposes)	Horton, William. (2000). *Designing Web-Based Training.* New York: Wiley.
User and Task Analysis for Interface Design	Excellent, in-depth discussion of analyzing user context for interface design	Hackos, JoAnn T., & Redish , Janice C. (1998). *User and Task Analysis for Interface Design.* New York: John Wiley & Sons.
UsableWeb	Index to usability resources on the Web	<http://www.usableweb.com>
Library of Congress Usability Testing	Simple but useful	<http://rs7.loc.gov/loc/webstyle/usabilit.html>
UPA	Usability Professionals Organization	<http://www.upassoc.org>
Handbook of Usability Testing	Methods and principles of usability testing	Rubin, Jeffrey. (1994). *Handbook of Usability Testing: How to Plan, Design, and Conduct Effective Tests.* New York: John Wiley & Sons.

University of Maryland's Usability Resource List	Extensive list of web-based resources for usability	<http://www.otal.umd.edu/guse/testing.html>
Usability at Microsoft	Descriptions, reports, and more on usability testing at Microsoft	<http://www.microsoft.com/usability>

Index

Accessibility, of web sites, 27
Active reading, 2
Ad hoc connections, structure for, 70
Alta Vista search engine, 37–38, 72, 96
Aspect ratio, of online and printed text, 12–13
Audiences, 1–2. *See also* Users
Automatic movement, as navigation device, 88, 97–99

Banners, 15, 105, 108, 109
Beta testing, 58–59
Bookmarking, sites with frames, 92–93
Browsers
    differences between, 23–25
    problems with multiple frames, 92–93
Button navigational devices, 87, 93

Categories, structuring, 68–69
CD-ROM games, 99
Cell phones, web-enabled, 25
Clustering techniques, 106, 109, 110
Color
    as design technique, 105–106
    of online and printed text, 14
Communication, and context, 21
Computer screen
    aspect ratio of, 13
    color range of, 14
    size and resolution of, 12
Content, web site, 4–5
Context
    impact on meaning, 21
    mental, 28–30
    physical, 27–28
    social and institutional, 30
    technical, 23–27

understanding user, 6–10, 42
    and usability testing, 53–54, 55–57
    worksheet for, 31–32

Design complexity, and user context, 8–9
Design sketches, for determining site structure, 73–83. *See also* Screen layout
Disabled users, and technical context, 27
Dreamweaver, 5

Embedded links. *See* In-text links
Expert users, structuring site for, 66–67, 72, 76, 77–78, 82

Feedback, for existing web sites, 46–49. *See also* User analysis and testing
Fixity, of printed text, 14
Fluidity, of online print, 14
Focus groups, 50–52
Forward/backward navigational device, 88, 95–97
Frames
    for grid patterns, 109
    as navigation device, 87, 90–93, 100
Free-form information
    in-text link for, 88
    search engines for, 71–72, 94, 100
FrontPage, 5
Full network structures, 71–73, 75

Goals, users', 33–40
    conflicting and contradictory, 37–38

Goals, users', *(continued)*
  long-term, 37
  short-term, 36
  and type of structure, 62
  worksheet for, 39–40
Google search engine, 72, 73
Graphic complexity
  and technical context, 22–23
  and user context, 8–9
Graphics
  and computer aspect ratio, 13
  for headings, 105–106
  placement of, 24–25
Grid elements, in screen layout,
  106–110

Headings, in screen layout, 105–106
Hierarchical structures
  hub and spoke, 69
  navigation devices for, 97, 100
  outlines, 68–69
  in screen layout, 102–106
HTML tables, 108–109
Hub and spoke structure, 62, 69, 71,
  75
Hypertext. *See* Online text

Index, web site, 4, 72, 97
Information, user
  methods for acquiring, 44–59
  needs sketch for, 76–78
  See also User analysis and testing;
  Users
Institutional contexts, 30, 31
Intermediate users, structuring site
  for, 76, 77, 79–80, 81–82
Internet Explorer, 23–25
Interviews, 50–52
In-text links, 11, 87, 88–90, 100
Intranet web sites, 27
IRC channels, 18

Language, and user context, 7–8, 9
Layout. *See* Screen layout
Linear structure

  navigation devices for, 95–96, 100
  with nodes, 67–68, 69, 73, 75
  with scrolling, 67, 68, 69, 75
Links
  in linear structure, 67–68
  and navigational device choice, 86
  overuse of, 36
  See also In-text links; Navigational
  devices
Location, as design technique,
  105–106
Long-term goals, 37
Lynx, 23–24, 93

Macrostructure, 61. *See also* Structure
Main page
  relating subpages to, 73, 105
  site name on, 105
Meaning, and context, 21
Mental context, 28–30, 31
Microstructure, 61. *See also* Structure
Monitoring, web site usability, 46–49,
  58
MOO spaces, 18
Multiple structures, 63, 65, 81

Navigation, 2-4
Navigational devices, 86
  automatic movement, 88, 97–99
  buttons, 87, 93
  defined, 2–4, 86
  forward/backward, up/down, pre-
  vious/next, 88, 95–97
  frames, 87, 90–93
  in-text link, 87, 88–90
  making decisions about, 99–100
  navigation bar, 87, 90
  for online and printed texts, 10–11
  progress bars, 49
  search engines, 88, 94–95
  table of contents, 88, 97
  types of, 86–88
Navigation bar, 87, 90, 100, 110
  fixed, 90–92
  as structural element, 71,82

Navigation-oriented site, 15
Netscape Navigator, 23–25
Network structures
    full, 71–73, 75
    navigation devices for, 100
    partial, 70–71, 75
Newspapers, online vs. print, 18
Nodes, linear structure with, 67–68,
    69, 73
Novice users, structuring site for, 66,
    76–77, 78–79, 81–82

Online text
    compared with printed text, 10–18
    embedded links in, 88–90
    navigational devices for, 96
    reader as "writer" of, 15–18
    structure of, 65, 67–68, 69
Outline structures, 64, 68–69, 75, 83

Palm Pilots, 25
Partial network structure, 70–71, 75
Participatory design, 52, 55–58
Participatory observation, 55–58
Physical contexts, 27–28, 31
Pop-up window, for user feedback, 46
Post-release testing, 58–59
Previous/next navigational device,
    88, 95–97, 100
Printed text
    compared with online text, 10–18
    structure of, 65
Printing, sites with frames, 92–93
Progress bar, 49
Public-access kiosk, 28

Random information. See Free-form
    information
Random sampling, 43, 45
Readers, 1–2. See also Users
Reading patterns
    and navigational device choice, 86
    online vs. printed text, 11, 15–18
    and screen layout, 105
Resolution, of text, 12

Revision, ongoing web site, 59
Sampling methods, 42
    random sampling, 43
    self-selected groups, 43
    targeted sampling, 44
Screen. See Computer screen
Screen layout
    design sketches for determining,
        79, 80, 81–82
    design techniques for, 105–110
    grid elements in, 106–110
    hierarchical structures in, 102–106
Scrollbars, in linear structure, 67, 68,
    69
Search engines, 37–38, 69, 83
    forward/backward buttons in,
        96–97
    as navigation device, 88, 94–95,
        100
    in network structures, 71–73
    problems with multiple frames, 93
Self-selected groups, 43, 46
Short-term goals, 36
Size
    as design technique, 105–106
    of text, 12
Social contexts, 30, 31
Splash pages, 97–98, 99, 102, 104
Structure(s)
    complexity of, and reader as
        "writer", 15–18
    defined, 2–4, 61
    design sketches for determining,
        73–83
    differences in online and printed
        text, 10–18
    for diverse users, 62, 65–67, 72,
        81–82, 83
    on ESPN's web site, 62–65
    graphical representation of, 75
    grid patterns, 106–110
    hierarchical, in screen layout,
        102–106
    hub and spoke, 62, 69, 71
    importance of, 102

Structure(s) *(continued)*
    linear, 67–68
    multiple, 63, 65, 81
    and navigational device choice, 86,
      99–100
    network, 70-73
    outline, 64, 68–69
    two levels of, 6
    types of, 65–73, 74
    worksheet for, 83–84
Subpages, relating to main page, 73,
    105
Surveys, 45–50
    for existing web sites, 46–49
    worksheet for, 49–50

Table of contents
    as navigation device, 88, 95, 97,
      100
    for online and printed texts, 11
Targeted sampling, 44
Technical contexts, 23–27, 31
Testing. *See* User analysis and testing
Text, differences in online and
    printed, 10–18. *See also* Online text
Time-based media, 98
Touch-screen display, 28

Up/down navigational device, 88,
    95–97
Usability, 2–4
Usability testing, 52–55

User analysis and testing
    beta testing, 58
    for determining site structure,
      76–83
    importance of, 41–42
    interviews and focus groups, 50–52
    limitations of, 57
    participatory design, 55, 56–57
    participatory observation, 55–56
    post-release testing, 58
    sampling methods for, 42–44
    surveys, 45–50
    usability testing, 52–55
User context, understanding, 6–10.
    See also Context
Users
    and content, 5
    defined, 1–2
    disabled, 27
    diverse needs of, 62, 65–67, 72,
      81–82, 83
    reading patterns of, 15–18
    See also Expert users; Intermediate
      users; Novice users
Users' goals. *See* Goals

Web site design, crucial issues in, 2–4
Web site design programs, 5
WebTV, 25
Workspace structure, 12
Writer, reader as, 15–18